Standard Grade | Foundation | General

English

Foundation Level Reading 2003
2003 Foundation Level Reading Text
2003 Foundation Level Reading Questions

General Level Reading 2003
2003 General Level Reading Text
2003 General Level Reading Questions

Foundation Level Reading 2004
2004 Foundation Level Reading Text
2004 Foundation Level Reading Questions

General Level Reading 2004
2004 General Level Reading Text
2004 General Level Reading Questions

Foundation Level Reading 2005
2005 Foundation Level Reading Text
2005 Foundation Level Reading Questions

General Level Reading 2005
2005 General Level Reading Text
2005 General Level Reading Questions

Foundation Level Reading 2006
2006 Foundation Level Reading Text
2006 Foundation Level Reading Questions

General Level Reading 2006
2006 General Level Reading Text
2006 General Level Reading Questions

Foundation Level Reading 2007
2007 Foundation Level Reading Text
2007 Foundation Level Reading Questions

General Level Reading 2007
2007 General Level Reading Text
2007 General Level Reading Questions

2005 Foundation/General/Credit Level Writing
2006 Foundation/General/Credit Level Writing
2007 Foundation/General/Credit Level Writing

Leckie×Leckie

© Scottish Qualifications Authority
All rights reserved. Copying prohibited. No part of this publication may be reproduced, stored in a retrieval system, or transmitted in any form or by any means, electronic, mechanical, photocopying, recording or otherwise.

First exam published in 2003.
Published by Leckie & Leckie Ltd, 3rd Floor, 4 Queen Street, Edinburgh EH2 1JE
tel: 0131 220 6831 fax: 0131 225 9987 enquiries@leckieandleckie.co.uk www.leckieandleckie.co.uk

ISBN 978-1-84372-508-4

A CIP Catalogue record for this book is available from the British Library.

Printed in Scotland by Scotprint.

Leckie & Leckie is a division of Huveaux plc.

Leckie & Leckie is grateful to the copyright holders, as credited at the back of the book, for permission to use their material.
Every effort has been made to trace the copyright holders and to obtain their permission for the use of copyright material.
Leckie & Leckie will gladly receive information enabling them to rectify any error or omission in subsequent editions.

2003 Reading | Foundation

[BLANK PAGE]

0860/401

NATIONAL
QUALIFICATIONS
2003

TUESDAY, 6 MAY
10.35 AM – 11.25 AM

**ENGLISH
STANDARD GRADE**
Foundation Level
Reading
Text

Read carefully the passage overleaf. It will help if you read it twice. When you have done so, answer the questions. Use the spaces provided in the Question/Answer booklet.

John, Me and the Lancashire Treasure

1 I learned the meaning of *gold fever* when I was thirteen — it came in the shape of thirty-three Roman coins dug out of the bed of a small stream on a West Lancashire farm.

2 A chance remark by a friend of my sister's that a hoard of coins had once been discovered about two miles from where I lived turned me, and my lifelong friend John Rimmer, into keen, young archaeologists. Our logic went: if 100 coins had been found there already then surely there must be a few more lying around undiscovered. There were, but getting at them was murder.

3 The trouble was that the Roman soldier, or whoever had originally owned them, had chosen the side of a stream in which to bury them. But unfortunately during the next nineteen hundred years or so the stream had slightly changed course until the coins were embedded in its bank or buried in the silt in the bottom.

4 When we first went coining it was the Easter holidays. Equipped with huge shovels and pans which we borrowed from the local farm we began the spine-bending task of shovelling silt from the bottom of the stream into a pan, carefully carrying the pan to a place where the water flowed more quickly, washing out the mud and then staring like fortune-tellers into tea leaves at the remaining collection of tiny pebbles for the dull coins we had been told about.

5 By mid-afternoon we were beginning to wonder whether some cruel joke had been played upon us and we took to catching tiddlers in our vacuum flasks, chasing the cows back from our site and hurling chunks of mud after a trespassing water rat. At tea-time, when our hearts were hardly in it, the boy from the local farm paid us a visit. It was he who had originally discovered the treasure.

6 "How many have you got?" he asked casually, leaning over the handlebars of his bicycle. "None," we answered dejectedly, half afraid even to look at him.

7 He grunted, climbed from his bicycle and clambered down the bank. "You're digging in the wrong place," he said. "You should be more over here." And taking my shovel from me he quickly filled the pan full of silt, washed it out and began to sift through the remains. Suddenly his hand shot forward like the tongue of a snake. "There you are," he said. "That's one!"

8 He passed me a dull piece of metal about the size of a five pence piece. It was a coin, but not much of a coin. "You have it," he said, "and dig in the right place next time." And with that he climbed back on his bike and pedalled away up the field. Putting the coin carefully into a purse we had brought for our anticipated treasure, we returned to our work with renewed enthusiasm. Before the day was out we had actually found a couple of our own, although none of them would have convinced a doubter. Nineteen hundred years had erased all their markings.

9 The next day we hit the jackpot. From virtually the first panning we pulled out three almost perfect coins, probably as clearly marked as when they had been originally buried. We had actually found treasure, proper treasure, with heads and names impressed upon it.

10 But suddenly the easy friendship which we had shared for years became stretched with tension as jealousy crept in.

11 We would peer together over the pan, each desperate to spot the next coin before the other. And now we began to make our own separate collections. We found the coins which had been overlooked, but, like a couple of gold-crazy prospectors, mutual distrust and envy had taken over.

12   For two weeks we worked that stream.

13   By now, of course, the whole river bank looked like something out of the Klondike, as heaps of rubble were tipped upon the grass after examination. We were less than pleased when the farmer's son came with the news that his father would like us to tidy up before we finished. By now we must have collected over twenty coins and we would pore over reference books in John's house trying to trace exactly what kind of coins we had found.

14   Then a strange thing happened: I lost one, and with it I lost interest. I know I had it on the bus going to school. But when I got there it had gone. John was livid. He was convinced I'd given it to the bus conductor by mistake.

15   All the fun of finding the coins was souring our friendship, so one day I just put all my share into a handkerchief, wrapped it up and gave it to my friend. "You'd better keep them," I said. "I don't trust myself not to lose the lot."

16   It was true, I didn't. And anyway, I had all kinds of new hobbies to be getting on with: there was chicken farming (all fifty died on me), mushroom growing, sword-collection (my mother eventually gave them to a house decorator) and rock and roll. The fun had been *finding* the coins. John was a much better bank than I was.

17   I went to see him a couple of years ago. He lives in New Zealand now and keeps them in a safe, all carefully labelled — apart from three very rare ones which apparently even puzzled the British Museum. And apparently people come from miles around to see his grand collection.

18   With great pride he carefully got them out for me and spread them across the dining table as we reminisced about who found which ones. At last, I asked nervously whether I might have one.

19   "One!" he said in astonishment. "You can take half of them. Choose any fifteen. They're yours. I've only been looking after them for you until you came to your senses."

20   I chose one. It was one I remembered finding. I still didn't trust myself with the rest. Apparently they're worth over £1,000 now and going up in value all the time.

21   It's a pretty wonderful thing to be thirteen years old and find buried treasure.

Adapted from an article by *Ray Connolly*

[*END OF PASSAGE*]

[BLANK PAGE]

Official SQA Past Papers: Foundation English 2003

FOR OFFICIAL USE

F

Total Mark

0860/402

NATIONAL QUALIFICATIONS 2003

TUESDAY, 6 MAY
10.35 AM – 11.25 AM

ENGLISH—
STANDARD GRADE
Foundation Level
Reading
Questions

Fill in these boxes and read what is printed below.

Full name of centre

Town

Forename(s)

Surname

Date of birth
Day Month Year

Scottish candidate number

Number of seat

NB Before leaving the examination room you must give this booklet to the invigilator. If you do not, you may lose all the marks for this paper.

SCOTTISH
QUALIFICATIONS
AUTHORITY

SAB 0860/402 6/32970

QUESTIONS

Write your answers in the spaces provided.

Look at Paragraphs 1 and 2.

1. Where were the Roman coins discovered?

   _____

2. **Write down two** reasons why the writer and his friend became "keen, young archaeologists".

   (i) _____

   (ii) _____

3. **Write down an expression** which tells you that the coins were difficult to get to.

   _____

Look at Paragraph 3.

4. (a) Where had the original owner of the coins buried them?

   _____

   (b) Why had the coins moved from where they were first buried?

   _____

   _____

Look at Paragraph 4.

5. **Write down two pieces** of equipment the boys used to help them find the coins.

   (i) _____

   (ii) _____

6. **Write down an expression** which suggests that looking for the coins was hard work.

   _____

7. Why do you think the writer uses the simile "staring like fortune-tellers into tea leaves"?

   _____

   _____

Look at Paragraphs 5 and 6.

8. Why were the boys beginning to think by mid-afternoon that someone had played a cruel joke on them?

   _____

9. Give **two reasons** why the visit of the local farm boy was important.

   (i) _____

   (ii) _____

10. **Write down the word** which describes how the boys were feeling about not finding coins.

    _____

Look at Paragraphs 7 and 8.

11. What does the expression "his hand shot forward like the tongue of a snake" tell you about how the boy moved when he discovered the coin?

    _____

12. **Write down two reasons** why the writer thought that it was "not much of a coin".

    (i) _____

    (ii) _____

[Turn over

13. Write down an expression which shows the effect that finding the coins had on the boys.

_____

Look at Paragraph 9.

14. Explain why the writer uses the expression "The next day we hit the jackpot".

_____

_____

Look at Paragraphs 10, 11, 12 and 13.

15. (a) Which word **best** describes how the boys began to feel towards each other as they found more and more coins?

   Tick (✓) the correct box.

Trusting	
Unselfish	
Suspicious	

   (b) Give a reason for your answer.

   _____

   _____

16. **Write down two things** which the boys did which show that they had become really interested in the coins.

   (i) _____

   (ii) _____

Look at Paragraphs 14, 15 and 16.

17. What effect did the loss of the coin have on the writer?

   _____

18. How did John think the coin had been lost?

   _____

   _____

19. **Write down two reasons** why the writer gave his coins to his friend John.

   (i) _____

   (ii) _____

20. Why is the word "*finding*" in italics?

   _____

   _____

Look at Paragraphs 17, 18, 19 and 20.

21. Where are the coins now kept?

   _____

   _____

22. Why were three of the coins not labelled?

   _____

   _____

[*Turn over for Questions 23 and 24 on Page six*

23. **Give two reasons** why, in your opinion, the writer chose only one coin.

(i) _____

(ii) _____

Think about the passage as a whole.

24. **Write down two things** that you have learned about "*gold fever*" from the passage.

(i) _____

(ii) _____

[*END OF QUESTION PAPER*]

2003 Reading | General

[BLANK PAGE]

0860/403

NATIONAL
QUALIFICATIONS
2003

TUESDAY, 6 MAY
1.00 PM – 1.50 PM

ENGLISH
STANDARD GRADE
General Level
Reading
Text

Read carefully the passage overleaf. It will help if you read it twice. When you have done so, answer the questions. Use the spaces provided in the Question/Answer booklet.

We're out for the Count

Catriona Marchant and her children discover that Dracula has a big stake in Romania's tourist industry.

1. The door creaked open. A draught of cold air blew up from the stairs to the dark crypt and the hairs on our arms stood on end. The faint light from the flickering candle disappeared, there was a muffled scream, a sound of running footsteps and then some raised voices.

2. My three brave boys looked at each other and Douglas, the middle one, ran from the room. The eldest, Matthew, who had been taunting his younger brothers about being scared five minutes earlier, went a bit white and looked like he was going to change his mind about the visit.

3. We were in Dracula's castle — sited on the remote Tihuta mountain pass where the Victorian Gothic novelist Bram Stoker based the home of his fictitious vampire — two days' carriage ride from Bistrita in northern Transylvania.

4. Downstairs was Count Dracula's coffin in a narrow vault, the walls painted with the dramatic scenes of human victims, wolves, skulls, skeletons and the black-cloaked monster himself, red blood dripping from his pointed fangs. So far on our Romanian holiday the only blood-sucking had been from the mosquitoes in Bucharest. Luckily we had decided to send their father down first as a guinea pig to test out how scary this experience was likely to be for our seven-, five- and two-year-olds.

5. After the screams from the crypt, Matthew decided he would opt for a tour with the light on and I agreed. Even so there was a certain nervousness as we went down the stairs. Suddenly, Matthew let out a blood-curdling scream and jumped a foot in the air. "I've just seen a horrible blue hand with long nails, round the side of that door," he screeched.

6. One vampire hand was quite enough for a seven-year-old. Time for a drink and an ice-cream. As we walked up to the main lobby there was "Vampire" red wine for sale, glass vials of red liquid, wooden stakes and probably some garlic stashed under the counter.

7. As these tacky souvenirs revealed, it wasn't the real Dracula's castle but Hotel Castel Dracula, a three-star hotel built in the mountains to service some nearby ski slopes. The architecture (1980s mock castle) reflected the Dracula movies but the setting amid the dramatic scenery of the Tihuta pass is stunning. The "castle" is circled by bats every night and the surrounding forests have more wild bears and wolves than anywhere else in Europe.

8. Bram Stoker's story has become mixed up with the historical facts as the novelist based his blood-sucking fictional vampire on the 15th century bloodthirsty Prince Vlad Tepes. Vlad was known fondly as Vlad the Impaler.

9. The tourist board makes the most of this confusion between fiction and history, as the worldwide fascination with Dracula lures many a visitor to the country. The most well known sights are the birthplace of Vlad Tepes at the beautiful town of Sighisoara and Bran Castle, commonly known as Dracula's Castle.

10. Bran Castle is certainly dramatic, perched on the edge of a rock peak, its ramparts standing out against the dark mountain backdrop. But as it was the former summer royal residence, parts of it inside seem rather cosy and welcoming. The ruined castle of Rasnov seems a more suitable location for a Dracula film, with 360-degree views of the Carpathian Mountains after a steep walk up the wooded mountain.

11. Matthew did his best to scare the tourists. He had been reading his Dracula books and dressed up in a black cloak, cut out some paper fangs and jumped round corners and down steps.

12. He gained more smiles and laughs than any signs of horror — but then it was a warm, sunny August day. He completed his vampire outfit by choosing wooden daggers for himself and Douglas from the busy craft market to protect us from any blood-sucking monsters that might come our way (apart from mosquitoes).

Cloak and dagger: Alistair and Matthew had a scream fooling around near the birthplace of Vlad Tepes, the "original Dracula"

13 Dracula's Kiss was an extremely alcoholic, bright scarlet drink. This fiery concoction must have contained a large quantity of the local plum brandy, known as palinca. I drank this at the birthplace of Vlad Tepes in Sighisoara. His house is now a restaurant which offers themed menus such as Dracula's tomato soup and fairly average food.

14 Not all the themed food given to the tourists on the hunt for Count Dracula is poor. One of the best and most exciting meals of the holiday was at the Count Dracula Club in Bucharest. Once the children got over the fear of the stuffed bears and stags on the walls and dog head skulls hanging from the ceiling, the food was fantastic — thick vegetable soup, polenta with stuffed cabbage leaves. The children drank blood orange juice and feasted on thick stew. Down in the cellar was the coffin, with the waiters dressed like vampires and acting for all they were worth.

15 Away from the crypts was hot summer sunshine: we swam in outdoor swimming pools and visited spas with bubbling warm salt lakes. We felt Romania would be a good place to revisit when the boys were older and could hike and camp in the Carpathian wilderness. The most memorable part of our visit to Romania was staying with a delightful family in Sighisoara who loved the children and treated them with kindness as they helped feed their chickens and cook special apple cake.

16 But if we leave the return visit too long things will have changed dramatically. A DraculaLand theme park is planned to be built by a German or American corporation in medieval Sighisoara next year.

17 Local opinion is divided. On the one hand, there is the desire for tourist money and on the other the realisation that the theme park will change the character of the small town forever. If the cobbled streets are lined with fast food chains offering "stakeburgers" and garlic bread — Dracula will be turning in his grave.

Adapted from an article by
Catriona Marchant

[END OF PASSAGE]

[BLANK PAGE]

FOR OFFICIAL USE

0860/404

NATIONAL
QUALIFICATIONS
2003

TUESDAY, 6 MAY
1.00 PM – 1.50 PM

ENGLISH
General Level
Reading
Questions

Total Mark

Fill in these boxes and read what is printed below.

Full name of centre

Town

Forename(s)

Surname

Date of birth
Day Month Year

Scottish candidate number

Number of seat

NB Before leaving the examination room you must give this booklet to the invigilator. If you do not, you may lose all the marks for this paper.

SCOTTISH QUALIFICATIONS AUTHORITY

SAB 0860/404 6/71570

Official SQA Past Papers: General English 2003

QUESTIONS

Write your answers in the spaces provided.

Look at Paragraph 1.

1. **In what two ways** does the writer create a frightening atmosphere in the opening sentence?

   (i) "The door creaked open"

   (ii) "...the hairs on our arms stood on end"

2. Explain fully what the writer suggests by using the word "flickering" when describing the candle.

   It isn't constantly glowing and is causing darkness in the room

Look at Paragraph 2.

3. "My three brave boys"

   Explain fully why this expression might be considered to be surprising.

   because five minutes earlier they were scared, and after the door creaking open they were scared

4. **Explain in your own words** how Matthew had been treating his brothers.

   He had been teasing his brothers for being scared

Look at Paragraph 3.

5. **Give two pieces of evidence** which suggest that Bram Stoker wrote the novel *Dracula* more than one hundred years ago.

   (i) "...his blood sucking fictional novel vampire on 15th century..."

   (ii) They also talk about people living in castles

6. Why does the writer use dashes in Paragraph 3?

   because he is changing the subject

Look at Paragraph 4.

7. "Downstairs was Count Dracula's coffin in a narrow vault, the walls painted with the dramatic scenes"

   In what ways does the writer convey the "dramatic scenes" in the vault?

   He lists the a description of the room and speaks about dramatic images

8. What effect does the writer create by using the expression "So far on our Romanian holiday the only blood-sucking had been from the mosquitoes"?

   The writer makes it sound like the holiday has been boring and petty "..the only blood-sucking had been from the mosquitoes

9. **In your own words** explain fully why their father was sent down first.

   To make sure the tour was suitable for the children and wasn't to scary

Look at Paragraphs 5, 6 and 7.

10. **Write down an expression** which shows that Matthew did not complete the tour.

    "One vampire hand was quite enough for the 7 yearold"

11. **In your own words** what is the writer's attitude to the various goods for sale in the hotel lobby?

    They are tacky and not worth buying

12. **In your own words** what is the writer's opinion of the setting of the Hotel Castel Dracula?

    It is just a fake and it is trying to copy the real Draculas castle

13. Why does the writer place the word "castle" in inverted commas?

    It isn't a real one and its just an imatation

Look at Paragraphs 8 and 9.

14. What was the real name of the original Dracula?

    Vlad Tepes

15. Explain **in your own words** how Romania benefits from "this confusion between fiction and history".

    Tourists pay for tours and souvenirs

Look at Paragraph 10.

16. What contrasting impressions does the writer give of Bran Castle?

    It is a good resemblance of Draculas Castle from a movie and but would also be a good place for a family to visit

Look at Paragraphs 11, 12 and 13.

17. "He gained more smiles and laughs than any signs of horror"

    Give two reasons why Matthew was an unconvincing vampire.

    He was just a young boy and had fangs made from paper

18. What does the expression "fiery concoction" suggest about the Dracula's Kiss drink?

    It is hot and has a kick to it

Look at Paragraph 14.

19. (a) **In your own words explain how** the boys felt at the start of their visit to the Count Dracula Club. **Why** did they feel this way?

    They were scared because of the stuffed animals

    (b) **Write down an expression** which clearly shows that the boys changed their attitude to the visit.

    "Once the boys children got over the fear" this shows the have got over it

Look at Paragraphs 15, 16 and 17.

20. What kind of holiday in Romania might the writer consider in the future?

    They would like to return but soon because it is changing into a theme park

21. (a) How does the writer feel about the changes planned for the tourist industry in Romania?

    The writer believes that the character of the town will change

    (b) Explain **in your own words** how the local people feel about the planned changes.

    It is divided some think it will be good for buisness but some think the character will change

    (c) "Dracula will be turning in his grave."
    Why does the writer finish off the final sentence in this way?

    The writer says this because he believes Dracula would think its wrong and would not like the change

[Turn over for Question 22 on *Page six*

Think about the passage as a whole.

22. "Catriona Marchant and her children discover that Dracula has a big stake in Romania's tourist industry."

    Explain fully what is appropriate about this sub-title.

    She has done research on this and has seen that the main attraction is Dracula

    2 1 0

[END OF QUESTION PAPER]

2004 Reading | Foundation

[BLANK PAGE]

0860/401

NATIONAL
QUALIFICATIONS
2004

WEDNESDAY, 5 MAY
10.35 AM – 11.25 AM

ENGLISH
STANDARD GRADE
Foundation Level
Reading
Text

Read carefully the passage overleaf. It will help if you read it twice. When you have done so, answer the questions. Use the spaces provided in the Question/Answer booklet.

In this extract the narrator and his brother are on an overnight camping and hunting trip when something unusual happens.

1   At some point I drifted off to sleep and when I woke I thought it was dawn. Then I realised the pale light coming through the canvas was moonlight. I was absolutely alert, and tense. Something had wakened me. I lay there, hardly daring to breathe. Then I heard a whisper, a low hiss of a whisper, outside the tent. It was calling my name.

2   Somebody was out there. My brother was breathing gently beside me, fast asleep. I simply listened. I don't know what I thought. I felt no fear, but still I was amazed to feel the tears trickling slowly down over my ears, as I lay staring upwards.

3   The whisper came again, my name. It seemed to be coming from about where the fire was.

4   Very carefully, partly not to waken my brother, partly not to let the voice know I was listening, I sat up, leaned forward, and tried to peep through the laced-up door of the tent. By holding the edges of the flaps slightly apart, I could see a tiny dot of red glow still in our campfire. Everything out there was drenched in a grey, misty light.

5   Somebody was standing beside the fire.

6   It was a person and yet I got the impression it was somehow not a person. Or it was a very small person. It looked like a small old woman, with a peculiar bonnet on her head and a long shawl. That was my impression. As I stared with all my might, trying to make out something definite, this figure drifted backwards into the shade of the trees. But the whisper came again:

7   "Come out. Quickly. There's been an accident."

8   I immediately knew it must be somebody from the farm. Surely it was the farmer's little old mother. That was how she knew we were here. The farmer had fallen down a well, or down a loft ladder, or a mad cow had crushed his ribs. Or he'd simply tumbled downstairs going to get his old mother a cup of tea because she couldn't sleep.

9   Something stopped me waking my brother. What I really wanted was to find out more. Who was this person? What was the accident? Anyway, it was my name that had been called. It must be me that was specially needed. I could come back and tell my brother later. Most of all, I wanted to see who this was.

10 I had gone to sleep in my clothes, to keep warm and for a quick start. So now I pulled on my boots. I unlaced the tent door at the bottom and crawled out. The grass was cold and soaking under my hands.

11 "Hurry," came the whisper from under the trees. "Hurry, hurry."

12 It seems strange, that I felt no fear. I was so sure that it was somebody from the farm, that I thought of no other possibility. Only huge curiosity, and excitement. Also, I felt quite important suddenly.

13 I went toward the voice, staring into the dark shade. The moon was past full but very hard and white. I wanted to get into the shade quickly, where I wouldn't be so visible.

14 But now the voice came again, from further up the wood. Yes, the voice was climbing towards the farm.

15 "Hurry," it kept saying. "Hurry up."

16 Beneath the trees, the slope was clear and grassy, without brambles or undergrowth. Easy going but steep, with that tough, slippery grass.

17 As I climbed, the voice went ahead. Very soon, I would see through the top of the wood. The bright night sky was piled with brilliant masses of snowy cloud, beyond the dark tree stems. I glimpsed the black outline now and again, the funny bonnet, climbing ahead, bobbing between the trees.

18 "Are you coming?" came the whisper again. "This way."

19 I saw her shape in the gap of the wall, clear against those snowy clouds. Then she had gone through it. It was now, as I came up towards the gap, sometimes grasping grass to help myself upwards, that I saw something else, bouncing and scrabbling under the wall, in a clear patch of moonlight.

20 A great slab of stone had fallen. Beside it sat a well-grown fox cub, staring up at me, panting. As I took this in, the cub suddenly started again, tugging and bouncing, jerking and scrabbling, without a sound, till again it crouched there, staring up at me, its mouth wide open, its tongue dangling, panting.

21 I could see now that it was trapped by one hind leg and its tail. They were pinned to the ground under the corner of the big slab.

22 The smell was overpowering, thick, choking, almost liquid, as if concentrated liquid scent had been poured over me, soaking my clothes and hands. I knew the smell of fox – the smell of frightened fox.

23 Then I looked up and saw the figure out there in the field, only five yards away, watching me. More than ever I could see it was a little old woman, with her very thin legs and her funny bonnet and shawl. She did not seem to be wanting me to go to the farm. She had brought me to this fox cub. She was probably some eccentric old lady who never slept, or slept only by day and spent the night roaming the hillsides, talking to owls and befriending foxes. She would have seen our camp. Probably some of those tracks had been hers, brushed through the dew around our tent. Now she had found the trapped cub, and not being strong enough to lift the slab, she had come to us. She wanted me to lift the slab and free the cub. She had not called my brother because she thought he might kill it. She must have watched us, and heard him speak my name.

24 My first thought was to catch the cub and keep it alive. But how could I hold it and at the same time lift the slab? It was a desperate, ferocious little thing. I could have wrapped it in my jersey, knotting the arms round it. But I didn't think of that. As I put my fingers under the other corner of the slab, the cub snapped its teeth at me and hissed like a cat, then struggled again, jerking to free itself.

25 With all my strength I was just able to budge the slab a fraction. But it was enough. As the slab shifted, the cub scrabbled and was gone – off down the wood like a rocket.

26 I looked up at the old lady, and this was my next surprise. The bare, close-cropped, moonlit field was empty. I walked out to where she had been. The whole wide field, under the great bare sky of moonlight, all made much brighter by that great bulging heap of snowy, silvery clouds, was empty. Not even a sheep. Absolutely nothing.

Adapted from *Deadfall* by Ted Hughes

[*END OF PASSAGE*]

[BLANK PAGE]

Official SQA Past Papers: Foundation English 2004

FOR OFFICIAL USE

F

Total Mark

0860/402

NATIONAL QUALIFICATIONS 2004

WEDNESDAY, 5 MAY 10.35 AM – 11.25 AM

ENGLISH STANDARD GRADE Foundation Level Reading Questions

Fill in these boxes and read what is printed below.

Full name of centre

Town

Forename(s)

Surname

Date of birth
Day Month Year

Scottish candidate number

Number of seat

NB Before leaving the examination room you must give this booklet to the invigilator. If you do not, you may lose all the marks for this paper.

SAB 0860/402 6/33320

SCOTTISH QUALIFICATIONS AUTHORITY

QUESTIONS

Write your answers in the spaces provided.

Look at Paragraph 1.

1. **Write down an expression** which shows that the boy was unsure of when he had fallen asleep.

   _____

2. What made the boy think that he had slept until dawn?

   _____

3. What did the boy hear and what was unusual about it?

   _____

4. **Write down two expressions** from Paragraph 1 which show how the boy was feeling.

   (i) _____

   (ii) _____

Look at Paragraphs 2 and 3.

5. "Somebody was out there." (Paragraph 2)

   Why does the writer use this short sentence here?

   _____

   _____

6. Why was the boy's brother unaware of what was happening?

   _____

Look at Paragraph 4.

7. **Write down two reasons** why the boy moved very carefully inside the tent.

   (i) _____

   (ii) _____

8. What was **the first thing** the boy saw when he peeped through the tent flap?

_____

9. "Everything out there was drenched in a grey, misty light."

Why does the writer use the word "drenched"?

_____

_____

Look at Paragraphs 5 to 8.

10. Write down three things the boy noticed about the person standing beside the fire.

(i) _____

(ii) _____

(iii) _____

11. Write down an expression from Paragraph 6 which tells you that the boy was concentrating on the figure.

_____

12. What important information did the figure give to the boy?

_____

Look at Paragraphs 9 to 11.

13. Write down three reasons the boy gives for not wakening his brother.

(i) _____

(ii) _____

(iii) _____

14. Why was it possible for the boy to get ready so quickly?

_____

[0860/402] *Page three* [Turn over

Look at Paragraphs 12 to 14.

15. **Write down two expressions** which tell you the boy was certain that it was someone from the farm.

    (i) _____

    (ii) _____

16. **In your own words** what reason does the boy give for getting into the shade quickly?

    _____

    _____

Look at Paragraphs 15 to 18.

17. **Write down an expression** which helps to make the meaning of "glimpsed" clear.

    _____

Look at Paragraphs 19 to 22.

18. In what **two different ways** does the writer make the trapped fox cub's panic clear in Paragraph 20?

    (i) _____

    (ii) _____

19. **In your own words** what was the boy's reaction to the smell of the fox?

    _____

    _____

Look at Paragraph 23.

20. What did the boy now realise about the little old lady's purpose in leading him there?

    _____

21. **Write down the word** from Paragraph 23 which the boy uses to describe the little old lady's odd behaviour.

    _____

22. **Write down two reasons** why she had chosen the boy to rescue the cub.

(i) _____

(ii) _____

Look at Paragraphs 24 to 26.

23. "... ferocious little thing." (Paragraph 24)

Write down two expressions from later in the paragraph which develop this idea.

(i) _____

(ii) _____

24. Why does the writer use the expression "off down the wood like a rocket" to describe the cub's movements?

_____

_____

Think about the passage as a whole.

25. Who do you think the old lady was? **Using evidence from the passage** give a reason for your answer.

_____

_____

_____

[END OF QUESTION PAPER]

FOR OFFICIAL USE

p2
p3
p4
p5
TOTAL MARK

2004 Reading | General

[BLANK PAGE]

0860/403

NATIONAL
QUALIFICATIONS
2004

WEDNESDAY, 5 MAY
1.00 PM – 1.50 PM

ENGLISH
STANDARD GRADE
General Level
Reading
Text

Read carefully the passage overleaf. It will help if you read it twice. When you have done so, answer the questions. Use the spaces provided in the Question/Answer booklet.

Pucker Way to Kiss a Hummingbird

Mark Carwardine puts on lipstick in Arizona for a wild encounter.

1   There's a rather embarrassing tradition in wildlife circles in certain parts of Arizona. Visiting naturalists are encouraged to try to "kiss" a wild hummingbird.

2   This is more of a challenge for men than it is for women – mainly because it involves wearing lots of red lipstick. A dress and high heels are optional, but the redder and thicker the lipstick the better. Hummingbirds drink nectar from flowers that are often bright red and have learned to associate this particular colour with food. They mistake your mouth for one of their favourite plants – at least, that's the theory.

3   Which is how I found myself high in the mountains of South-East Arizona, with puckered lips pointing sky-ward and a crowd of bemused onlookers egging me on.

4   My home for a couple of days was Beatty's Guest Ranch near the Mexico border. Run by Tom and Edith Beatty, the ranch is nearly 6,000ft above sea level, nestling between two enormous peaks, with spectacular views down the valley to the desert below.

5   According to the South-Eastern Arizona Bird Observatory, it is the hottest hummingbird-watching spot in the state. Thousands of "hummers" arrive in April and May and stay until early October. No fewer than 15 different species are found here on a regular basis.

6   Dozens of special hummingbird feeders, looking like upside-down jam jars, are dotted around the ranch. Hanging from trees, bushes, fences and buildings they are full of a simple magic potion (four parts water, one part white sugar) similar to the nectar of hummingbird flowers. Tom and Edith keep the feeders topped up, getting through a mind-boggling 550 2lb bags of sugar in a typical year.

7   There were two feeders outside my bedroom window in the turn-of-the-century self-catering cabin on the forest edge (not a good place to stay if you've seen *Friday The 13th* or *The Blair Witch Project*, but idyllic in every other sense).

8   I will never forget pulling back the curtains on the first morning. There were hummingbirds everywhere, whizzing backwards and forwards past the window like demented bees. Sometimes they paused in front of the sugar-water to feed, either perching or hovering with the immaculate precision of experienced helicopter pilots.

9   Apparently, it's possible to see as many as ten species at the ranch in just half an hour. But even when they stayed still for more than a few moments I had no idea which was which. As they moved around, their colours changed in relation to the angle of the sun. Bird identification is hard enough at the best of times, but this was ridiculous.

10   Take a male hummingbird, for example. When you look at it face-to-face its throat is a fiery scarlet red. But as it turns away the colour shifts – first to orange, then yellow, then blackish-brown and then green. Try identifying that in a hurry, before it turns

SUMMER SPECTACLE:
Thousands of hummingbirds arrive in Arizona every year

into a blur and helicopters away.

11 I think there were Anna's hummingbirds, black-chinned, broad billed, blue-throated, magnificent, red and violet-crowned that morning, but I'm not entirely sure. Later, I asked other bird-watchers about similar-looking hummers around "their" feeding station, but they weren't sure either. I left them bickering over the difference between the sapphire blue throat of a broad-bill and the cobalt blue throat of a blue-throat.

12 The biological advantage of changing colour is that the birds can control the way they look. If a male wants to impress a female he shows his best side, but if he wants to hide from a predator he merely turns away and almost disappears among the greenery.

13 According to Sheri Williamson, hummingbird expert and co-founder of the South-Eastern Arizona Bird Observatory, you can tell them apart by the sound of their wings. Broad-tailed hummingbirds, for example, have a metallic trill to their wingbeats, while male black-chinned hummingbirds make a dull, flat whine.

14 Sheri took me to see a hummingbird in the hand. There's a ringing station, or banding station as they call it in the States, at nearby Sierra Vista. It's open to the public and every weekend the observatory staff rig up a mist-net trap with a tasty-looking sugar-water feeder in the middle. Whenever a hummingbird dares an investigatory hover, a burly member of the observatory team rushes forward, waving his arms around, and ushers the unfortunate bird inside.

15 We caught lots of hummingbirds that day. One was a female black-chinned that squealed when she was caught. It was hard to tell whether this was out of fear or anger ("How could I, so fleet of wing, be caught by this enormous fool?"). We found her abdomen distended with an enormous egg, which Sheri guessed would be laid before nightfall.

16 For a brief moment, I actually held the delicate bundle of feathers in my hand, and was so nervous about squeezing too hard that she escaped. After hovering above us for a moment, she made a bee-line for the bushes.

17 Hovering hummingbirds draw crowds of naturalists from all over the world to South-East Arizona, but hovering does have one major drawback. Pound for pound, beating your wings 70 times per second uses more energy than any other activity in the animal kingdom. Living life in the fast lane means hummingbirds need a continuous supply of fuel.

18 A typical hummingbird eats around half its own weight in energy-rich nectar every day. To do that it has to keep others away from its favourite foodplants. I spent many hours watching them battle it out at feeding stations. Far from being all sweetness and light, they are little fighter pilots. If they were the size of ravens it wouldn't be safe to walk in the woods.

19 Before I left, there was one thing I had to do. Dutifully, I put on bright red lipstick, took a mouthful of sugar-water, sat back, puckered my lips . . . and waited. Within 30 seconds two hummingbirds came to investigate. Others soon followed.

20 I sat there for an eternity not daring to move. No hummingbird actually drank sugar-water from my mouth (who can blame them?), but several did hover so close I could feel their wingbeats against my cheeks.

21 Strangely, the encounter was every bit as impressive as rubbing shoulders with mountain gorillas in the wilds of Africa or performing slow-motion underwater ballets with dolphins in the Bahamas.

22 Even better, my biggest worry came to nothing – the red lipstick wiped off.

(*Adapted from an article by Mark Carwardine*)

[END OF PASSAGE]

FOR OFFICIAL USE

G

Total Mark

0860/404

NATIONAL QUALIFICATIONS 2004

WEDNESDAY, 5 MAY
1.00 PM – 1.50 PM

ENGLISH
STANDARD GRADE
General Level
Reading
Questions

Fill in these boxes and read what is printed below.

Full name of centre

Town

Forename(s)

Surname

Date of birth
Day Month Year

Scottish candidate number

Number of seat

NB Before leaving the examination room you must give this booklet to the invigilator. If you do not, you may lose all the marks for this paper.

SCOTTISH QUALIFICATIONS AUTHORITY

SAB 0860/404 6/71420

QUESTIONS

Write your answers in the spaces provided.

Look at Paragraphs 1 and 2.

1. **Write down a word** from Paragraph 1 that suggests naturalists might be reluctant to kiss a hummingbird.

   embarrasing

2. Why are the hummingbirds attracted to someone wearing bright red lipstick?

   The humming birds drink nectar from red flowers so they think red is food

3. Why do you think the writer uses the word "theory" in Paragraph 2?

   It can't really be proven its just a suggestion why

Look at Paragraphs 3 and 4.

4. Where **exactly** did the writer first meet the hummingbirds?

   In South-East Arizona on Beatty's guest Ranch

Look at Paragraphs 5 and 6.

5. Thousands of "hummers" (Paragraph 5)

   Why has the writer put the word "hummers" in inverted commas?

   It is a sort of nickname and isn't their real name

6. "Hanging from trees, bushes, fences and buildings they are full of a simple magic potion . . . flowers." (Paragraph 6)

   Identify and comment on the effect of **two features** of the structure of this sentence.

   (i) *The writer lists where they put them this makes it sound like they have many places to put them*

   (ii) *He links the sentences.*

7. **Write down an expression** from Paragraph 6 which tells you that the writer is surprised by the amount of sugar used.

   Mind boggling

Look at Paragraphs 7 and 8.

8. What do the expressions "whizzing" and "like demented bees" tell you about the movement of the hummingbirds?

   They are moving around rapidly and crazily because they can easily fly into something

9. **Write down an expression** which shows that the writer admires the flying skills of the hummingbird.

   immaculate precission

Look at Paragraphs 9 and 10.

10. **In your own words** write down **two** reasons why the writer found bird identification "ridiculous".

    (i) *they moved around to fast to really see*

    (ii) *according to the angle of the bird to the sun the colours changed*

Look at Paragraphs 11 and 12.

11. What does the writer's use of the word "bickering" tell you about his attitude to the bird watchers?

They are argumentative

12. **In your own words** give **two** reasons why hummingbirds change their colour.

(i) To stand out to males/females

(ii) to blend into their surroundings to hide from prey

Look at Paragraphs 13 to 15.

13. How does Sheri Williamson tell the difference between hummingbirds?

She tells them apart from the sound of their wings

14. Comment on the writer's use of the expression "hummingbird in the hand".

It lets you know he is scared to have it in his hand but is also amazed

15. "Whenever a hummingbird dares an investigatory hover, a burly member of the observatory team rushes forward, waving his arms around" (Paragraph 14)

How does this description create effective contrasts?

(i) The hummingbird and the member of the observatory are both waving their arms around

(ii) They are both daring

Look at Paragraph 16.

16. What does the expression "I actually held" tell you about how the writer felt when he held the hummingbird?

He was amazed to be holding the hummingbird

Look at Paragraphs 17 and 18.

17. "Living life in the fast lane means hummingbirds need a continuous supply of fuel." (Paragraph 17)

Explain the effectiveness of this image.

if they are constantly moving and its always fast then they will be burning alot of energy and they will need more fuel to be able to do this

18. In your own words, what **two** new impressions does the writer give of the hummingbird in Paragraph 18?

It eats alot of food and it will fight for its food

Look at Paragraphs 19 to 22.

19. "Dutifully, I put on bright red lipstick . . . puckered my lips . . . and waited." (Paragraph 19)

Identify and comment on any **one feature** of structure **or** punctuation in this sentence.

He spread out what he done giving a list this gives the effect that he done it reluctantly

20. Write down an expression from Paragraph 20 which tells us the writer felt he waited for a long time.

an eternity

21. In your own words what does the writer's use of the word "Strangely" tell you about his reaction to the encounter with the hummingbirds?

He wasn't expecting this to happen

[Turn over for Questions 22 and 23 on *Page six*

Think about the passage as a whole.

22. From the passage **write down an example** of the writer's use of humour.

    Explain why it is effective.

    He used lipstick to try to attract the humming birds. He also mentions that they wear skirts and high heels

23. Overall how do you think the writer feels about his experience with the humming-birds?

    Support your answer by referring to the passage.

    He really enjoyed studying them and was touched "every bit as impressive as rubbing shoulders with mountain gorillas."

[END OF QUESTION PAPER]

2005 Reading | Foundation

[BLANK PAGE]

0860/401

NATIONAL
QUALIFICATIONS
2005

WEDNESDAY, 4 MAY
10.35 AM – 11.25 AM

ENGLISH
STANDARD GRADE
Foundation Level
Reading
Text

Read carefully the passage overleaf. It will help if you read it twice. When you have done so, answer the questions. Use the spaces provided in the Question/Answer booklet.

1   When he first woke up, Pete Smeaton was sure he was still dreaming.

2   Then he opened his eyes and knew that it had really happened. He was lying in a sleeping bag on the floor of a room in his new home. A home he had never set eyes on before.

3   And Jenny was crying.

4   At least some things never changed.

5   Pete sat up stiffly and looked around. Whatever room he was in was furnished with nothing but packing cartons stacked one on top of the other. He couldn't tell if the room was large or small because all he could see were boxes, labelled in his mother's hasty scrawl:

Kitchen, My room, Hall, Pete, Jenny.

6   He remembered the hurried squeak of the marker pen on the boxes as the carrier waited to transport them up from London. That was just yesterday.

7   Even muffled by packing cartons, Jenny's cry was shrill and piercing. Pete groaned and flopped back on his sleeping bag. He closed his eyes and put his hands over his ears. The crying grew louder. Pete opened one eye, as Jenny was shoved into his arms.

8   "Take her, will you, so I can at least go to the toilet on my own. If I put her down she'll be sick. This new place is giving her the heebie-jeebies. She was up all night."

9   Pete's mother left him with the hot, open-mouthed bundle that was his baby sister. Three months old and more hassle than twenty Petes had ever been, according to Mrs Smeaton.

10 Pete stared into the tiny, furious face.

11 "Hel–lo noisy," he said slowly. Secretly, he loved the feeling of Jenny when he held her although he would never admit that out loud to anyone. No way!

12 Hearing Pete's voice, Jenny stopped crying instantly. Pete felt her body relax in his arms.

13 "Why d'you always stop crying for me, you little monkey?" Pete whispered on Jenny's downy head. "You should give Mum a break."

14 Fitting Jenny expertly in the crook of one arm, Pete levered himself up from the floor.

15 "C'mon let's see what this place is like, Jenny. Time to explore."

16 The floorboards felt rough and chilly under Pete's feet. Snuggling Jenny close he went out into the hallway.

17 "Must have slept in the lounge," Pete figured. He was downstairs and the only other room on this floor was a large square kitchen with a small scullery. Beyond lay a wild-looking garden.

18 "It's a jungle out there, Jenny," said Pete in an American accent. "Better wait till I'm armed before I investigate."

19 Upstairs, on the half landing of the house there was a bathroom and one huge empty bedroom. The morning sun streamed through its emptiness illuminating the specks of dust which danced in such numbers that the room appeared in soft focus.

20 Pete stood in the centre of this room and knew that he wanted it to be his. It was at least three times the size of his old bedroom in London.

21 Quickly, he planned where he would put his books and lean his guitar. His bed would fit perfectly in that corner over there, and if his desk fitted under the window he'd be able to look outside and daydream while he was supposed to be doing his homework.

22 There'd be enough room for all his friends to stay overnight if they brought their sleeping bags.

23 "We could have a midnight feast and make up all those songs that drive Mum mad and . . ."

24 Pete was whispering excitedly to Jenny. Then he remembered where he was now:

25 "What an idiot. What friends?" he said bitterly to Jenny. "Don't know anyone here, do I? Never even heard of Clydebank before in my life. Don't even know what bloomin' school I'll be going to."

26 Pete stared into Jenny's blue unblinking eyes.

27 "You're lucky. Bet we'll be back in London by the time you need any friends. How am I going to meet anyone here?"

28 Pete leaned his forehead despondently on the glass and stared down at the garden. It really did look like a jungle. An expanse of unruly grasses weaved before Pete, reaching down to a ramshackle brick outbuilding. Beyond that, the boundary of the garden was drawn by a row of mature trees and bushes.

29 "It's huge," thought Pete, who had never lived in a house with a garden before. He had to admit—grudgingly—that this garden looked big enough for a decent game of football. It was his birthday next week. Maybe he'd ask for goalposts instead of that portable CD player he had his eye on.

30 Pete gazed out the window and saw himself running out onto the grass heading a crowd of boys:

31 "Good pass, Pete."

32 "Here, over to me, Pete."

33 "Yeah, nice one, Pete."

34 "Pete, Pete."

35 "Pete? Where on earth have you gone?"

36 Mrs Smeaton's irritation interrupted his daydream.

37 "What you doing with her now? It's all dusty up here." She shuddered, "Ugh! And chilly."

38 Mrs Smeaton yanked Jenny from Pete's arms. She was asleep, a smug little smile playing over her lips.

39 "Now look what you've done," Mrs Smeaton's voice rose in frustration. "I wanted to feed her first."

40 Pete shrugged, "Sorry, Mum. She was awake two minutes ago. Honest." He was going to add, "Got the magic touch, haven't I?" but something about his mum's pinched face and tired, shaky voice made him stop. She looked as though she was going to start crying again. He really hated that. Never could get used to it, even though she cried all the time these days. Her tears made Pete feel panicky and scared.

41 Quickly he asked, "Mum, can I have this room if you and Dad don't want it?"

42 "Do what you like," snapped the answer. "Won't make any difference to me. I don't sleep these days with this one yammering all the time. Someone in this family might as well use one of the bedrooms to get some rest."

43   The bitterness in his mother's voice made Pete wince. He stood at the door of his new room watching her slump wearily downstairs with Jenny in her arms. There was a horrible tight feeling inside his chest.

44   By the time Mrs Smeaton had reached the bottom stair, Jenny was wailing.

45   "Oh, for goodness' sake," Pete heard his mother sigh, as she carried Jenny through to the kitchen, slamming the door behind her so hard that the whole house shook.

46   Then the wailing became louder. And louder still. It turned into sobbing. Huge, uncontrollable sobbing. Pete stood with his hand on the door knob and listened.

47   "Mum?"

48   Pete was more taken aback by the power of the crying than by the crying itself. Surely it wasn't Jenny? It was much too powerful. Whoever was crying was much closer than the kitchen downstairs. And it sounded like a child. Right next to Pete.

Adapted from *Think Me Back* by Catherine Forde

[*END OF PASSAGE*]

Official SQA Past Papers: Foundation English 2005

FOR OFFICIAL USE

F

Total Mark

0860/402

NATIONAL QUALIFICATIONS 2005

WEDNESDAY, 4 MAY 10.35 AM – 11.25 AM

ENGLISH STANDARD GRADE Foundation Level Reading Questions

Fill in these boxes and read what is printed below.

Full name of centre

Town

Forename(s)

Surname

Date of birth
Day Month Year

Scottish candidate number

Number of seat

NB Before leaving the examination room you must give this booklet to the invigilator. If you do not, you may lose all the marks for this paper.

SCOTTISH QUALIFICATIONS AUTHORITY

SAB 0860/402 6/33170

QUESTIONS

Write your answers in the spaces provided.

Look at Paragraphs 1 to 4.

1. What was Pete's first thought when he woke up?

   that he was still dreaming.

2. What important event had just happened in Pete's life?

   he was in a new house.

3. "At least some things never changed."

   What does this sentence suggest?

   that Jenny cried alot.

Look at Paragraphs 5 and 6.

4. "mother's hasty scrawl:"

   (a) Give **two** reasons why the writer uses this expression to describe the writing on the boxes.

   (i) It had been done quickly
   (ii) It was untidy.

   (b) **Write down one word** from Paragraph 6 which continues this idea.

   hurried

Look at Paragraph 7.

5. **Write down two words** which describe Jenny's cry.

   Shrill   piercing

6. How did Pete feel about Jenny's crying?

he felt annoyed

Look at Paragraphs 8 to 10.

7. Give two reasons why Pete's mother asked him to hold the baby.

(i) wanted to go to the toilet

(ii) stop her being sick

8. Write down an expression which tells you that Pete had been an easier baby than Jenny.

more hassle than twenty petes

Look at Paragraphs 11 to 13.

9. Look at the final sentence of Paragraph 11.

How does the writer show Pete's strong feelings through

(i) sentence structure? they were short sentences.

(ii) punctuation? had exclamation mark

10. How did hearing Pete's voice affect Jenny?

stopped her crying

11. Write down the expression which shows that Pete felt sorry for his mum.

give mum a break

[Turn over

Look at Paragraphs 14 to 19.

12. **Write down one word** which shows that Pete was good at looking after his little sister.

    [expertly]

13. "Snuggling Jenny close" (Paragraph 16)

    Why did Pete do this?

    to stop her from getting cold.

Look at Paragraphs 20 to 25.

14. Write down any **three** things which Pete liked about the room.
    (i) bigger than his other room
    (ii) have sleepovers
    (iii) had a place for all his things

15. "We could have a midnight feast and make up all those songs that drive Mum mad and . . ." (Paragraph 23)

    Why did Pete not finish what he was saying?

    because he had no friends.

Look at Paragraphs 26 to 28.

16. **Write down the word** which shows that Pete thought there was no hope of having friends in his new home.

    [despondently]

17. Write down **three expressions** which tell you that the garden had not been looked after.

(i) _like a jungle_

(ii) _ramshackle_

(iii) _unruly_

Look at Paragraphs 29 to 34.

18. While daydreaming about the garden Pete imagined himself to be:

a football player ✓

a football referee ☐

a football fan ☐

Tick (✓) the correct box.

Look at Paragraphs 35 to 40.

19. "Mrs Smeaton's irritation interrupted his daydream." (Paragraph 36)

Write down two words from later **in this section of the passage** which develop the idea that Mrs Smeaton was angry.

yanked   _frustration_

20. What **three** things stopped Pete from continuing to answer his mother back?

(i) _pinched face_

(ii) _tired_

(iii) _shaky voice_

Look at Paragraphs 41 to 48.

21. "Mum, can I have this room if you and Dad don't want it?" (Paragraph 41)

Why did Pete ask his mum this question at this time?

distract her.

[Turn over for Questions 22 to 24 on *Page six*]

22. Write down three expressions which the writer uses to show that Pete's mother was still angry.

(i) do what you like

(ii) snapped

(iii) bitterness

23. "Surely it wasn't Jenny?" (Paragraph 48)

What **two** things made Pete think this?

(i) to close

(ii) powerful

Think about the passage as a whole.

24. Tick (✓) **two words** which you think best describe Pete's character.

Give evidence from the passage to support your choices.

Caring ✓

Imaginative ☐

Moody ☐

Sensitive ☐

(i) he cares for his sister — loved the feeling of Jenny

(ii) _____

[END OF QUESTION PAPER]

FOR OFFICIAL USE

p2
p3
p4
p5
p6

TOTAL MARK

[BLANK PAGE]

2005 Reading | General

[BLANK PAGE]

0860/403

NATIONAL
QUALIFICATIONS
2005

WEDNESDAY, 4 MAY
1.00 PM – 1.50 PM

ENGLISH
STANDARD GRADE
General Level
Reading
Text

Read carefully the passage overleaf. It will help if you read it twice. When you have done so, answer the questions. Use the spaces provided in the Question/Answer booklet.

Dazzled by the Stars

Our love affair with fame may be bad for our health, according to new research. **John Harlow** reports on "celebrity worship syndrome".

1 Under her bed Katherine Hicks keeps six years of yellowing newspaper clippings about the former pop band Boyzone, and 70 videos of their performances. There might have been more if her attention had not moved on to Westlife, another pop sensation.

2 In one year she has spent £3,000 to watch Westlife perform 17 times, and is such a regular concert fan that she believes the band now recognise her as an acquaintance, if not a friend.

3 She has fixed her sights on a new star: David Sneddon, first winner of the television show Fame Academy. She cornered Sneddon at two television appearances, though it is early days in her "acquaintance" with him. Yet she felt forced to defend him indignantly against a TV presenter who, she thought, had not shown Sneddon sufficient respect.

4 Hicks is no deluded young teen: she is a 28-year-old electrical engineer. But she freely admits to an "addiction" to the latest musical sensations. "I have an obsessive nature. Anything I do is full-on, but it has never caused me problems," she said last week. "I don't do anything I cannot afford, and I don't ring in sick at work to get time off."

5 She is no stalker or obsessive; she is just "fascinated by the real personas of these people". Though she likens her behaviour to an "addiction rather than an illness", she sees nothing odd in it.

6 "Other people think I am ill or sad," she said, "but I am not missing out on anything."

7 Psychologists, who are taking an increasing interest in the effects of celebrity culture, might disagree. As Anglo-American research published last week reveals, our relationship with celebrities is more complicated than we realise. The strength of our interest in celebrities, say academics, may affect our mood.

8 Lynn McCutcheon, of DeVry University in Florida, John Maltby, of Leicester University, and two colleagues will publish a book next year exposing the psychological needs and drives behind celebrity worship.

9 But initial results of research they have conducted show that about a third of people suffer from what the researchers call "celebrity worship syndrome" and it affects their mental wellbeing.

10 It raises a troubling question: in the era of "industrialised fame", is hero worship bad for you?

11 Perhaps we should blame the start of it on Alexander the Great who, more than 2,000 years ago, exploited to the full the idea of the beautiful "god-king".

12 But if celebrity has been a cultural phenomenon for centuries, why should it have become a problem now? McCutcheon and Maltby believe the scale of it has made a huge jump in recent years. The average westerner is now exposed to hundreds of star images every day, through advertising, broadcasting, fashion, the internet and innumerable other forms.

13 Though sales of some celebrity magazines are slipping, figures show that new publications are thriving. In America, the thirst for star images is so strong that one photographer was recently paid £70,000 for a single picture.

14 David Beckham is now so famous that one paper set out on a humorous quest to find someone who did not know who he was: they finally tracked down an innocent in the Saharan city of Timbuktu.

15 The rapid growth of fan-based internet sites spreads gossip, the lifeblood of celebrity, at lightning speed. There are

more than 100,000 sites dedicated to Madonna alone.

16   Such a speedy development has prompted the academics to create the celebrity attitude scale. Using a series of questions designed to gauge personality and the level of interest in celebrities, they surveyed 700 people.

17   Most were just casually interested in stars. But one in five people displayed a determined interest. They even rearrange their social lives, for example, to follow their chosen celebrity.

18   Some 10% of people displayed such "intense-personal" attitudes towards celebrities that they showed signs of addiction.

19   It can lead to extreme actions. On both sides of the Atlantic, some fans have resorted to plastic surgery to look more like their heroes. A Scottish actor had himself turned into a Pierce Brosnan lookalike and admits he now often walks and talks like 007.

20   Dr Nicholas Chugay, a Beverly Hills surgeon, has turned various Californians into Elvis Presley or Cher. "I have had to turn some people away because I do not feel it would be good for them to let such worship take over their lives," said Chugay.

21   BUT it may not be all that bad. Indeed, other academics argue that the likes of Beckham and Madonna are even good for you. They say that celebrity culture is based on sound reasons: by watching and imitating our so-called betters, whether it be in clothes or habits, we learn to flourish in human society.

22   Francisco Gil-White, of Pennsylvania University, argues we need celebrities to show us the road to success. He says they provide the educational and entertaining fables once sought in fairy tales.

23   "It makes sense to copy winners, because whoever is getting more of what everybody wants, and in this society this includes media attention, is probably using successful methods to get it."

24   But though some role models, such as Gareth Gates, the singer, and Tiger Woods, the golfer, can maintain they are blazing a trail for others to follow, can less worthy idols cause damage? Nancy Salzburg, who is researching charisma at San Diego University, said bad idols can cause trouble for their followers.

25   Choose well and there are benefits in celebrity, says Maltby. "It may help people to develop a relationship with and understand the world. If you admire someone like David Beckham, for example, and follow his dietary regime and the way he plays football, there can be a positive outcome in doing that."

26   Mark Griffiths, a professor of psychology at Nottingham Trent University, agrees.

27   "It was quite clear that for fans their idols formed a healthy part of their life," he said. "It was a way of raising their self-esteem.

28   What has happened is that people are not so religious and they don't look up to political and religious leaders any more. They have been replaced by the David Beckhams and the pop stars and film stars. That's who you see on the walls of teenagers' rooms because these are the people they look up to and admire."

Adapted from an article by
John Harlow

[END OF PASSAGE]

[BLANK PAGE]

Official SQA Past Papers: General English 2005

FOR OFFICIAL USE

G

Total Mark

0860/404

NATIONAL QUALIFICATIONS 2005

WEDNESDAY, 4 MAY 1.00 PM – 1.50 PM

ENGLISH
STANDARD GRADE
General Level
Reading
Questions

Fill in these boxes and read what is printed below.

Full name of centre

Town

Forename(s)

Surname

Date of birth
Day Month Year

Scottish candidate number

Number of seat

NB Before leaving the examination room you must give this booklet to the invigilator. If you do not, you may lose all the marks for this paper.

SCOTTISH QUALIFICATIONS AUTHORITY

SAB 0860/404 6/70470

QUESTIONS

Write your answers in the spaces provided.

Look at Paragraphs 1 and 2.

1. What evidence is there to suggest that Katherine Hicks was a keen fan of Boyzone?

   She keeps six years of newspaper clipping and 70 videos from their of performances under her bed

2. **Write down three key facts** which clearly show that Katherine Hicks is now a keen Westlife fan.

   (i) *She has spent £3,000 on them in a year*
   (ii) *Seen them perform 17 times*
   (iii) *She believes the recognise her as a friend now*

Look at Paragraph 3.

3. Why do you think the writer uses the expression "fixed her sights"?

   She has chosen to view someone else and has chosen a new star to follow

4. "early days in her "acquaintance" with him"

   Why has the writer put the word "acquaintance" in inverted commas?

   She isn't really their acquaintance, this is just the way she sees herself to them

5. What do the words "forced" and "indignantly" in Paragraph 3 tell you about Katherine's reactions to the TV presenter's treatment of David Sneddon?

   The TV presenter didn't give him any respect and was in his face

Look at Paragraphs 4 to 6.

6. "Hicks is no deluded young teen: she is a 28-year-old electrical engineer." (Paragraph 4)

   What does this statement tell you about the writer's attitude towards Katherine's behaviour?

   She behaves like a teenager

7. (a) Which of the following best describes Katherine's attitude towards her "addiction"?

   Tick (✓) the appropriate box.

   Concerned ☐

   Guilty ☐

   Relaxed ☑

   (b) **Quote an expression** to support your answer.

   "She admits freely to "addiction".."

Look at Paragraphs 7 to 10.

8. **Give three reasons** why psychologists are showing an increasing interest in "celebrity culture".

   (i) _"The strength of our interest in celebrities, say academics, may affect our mood_

   (ii) _needs and drives behind celebrity worship_

   (iii) _"celebrity worship syndrome"_

9. Explain why the writer ends Paragraph 10 with a question.

   To allow the reader to think about it and come to their own conclusion

Look at Paragraphs 11 to 14.

10. Who does the writer suggest is to blame for the start of hero worship?

   Alexander the great

11. **Quote an expression** which shows that celebrity worship is nothing new.

   ".. If celebrity worship has been a cultural phenomenon for centuries."

12. **In your own words** explain why the scale of hero worship has made a huge jump in recent years.

   Many papers, TV shows and Internet sites are based on these things so people are fascinated

13. What does the word "thirst" suggest about the American attitude towards celebrity gossip?

   It thrives on this and their is never enough

14. Why do you think the writer includes the information about the quest in Paragraph 14?

   To show that people are so well known even on the otherside of the world

Look at Paragraphs 15 to 18.

15. What has helped to spread celebrity gossip at great speed?

   Internet sites

16. **In your own words** what is the "celebrity attitude scale" designed to reveal?

The attitude of the public towards celebrities and groups

Look at Paragraphs 19 and 20.

17. In what **two** ways does the writer show the extent of celebrity "addiction"?

(i) Some fans have resorted to plastic surgery

(ii) They have changed their behaviour to be like them

Look at Paragraphs 21 to 24.

18. Why does the writer put the word "BUT" in capital letters at the beginning of Paragraph 21?

He is changing his view towards it and the way he is writing about them

19. In the opinion of Francisco Gil-White, what important influence have celebrities replaced?

They have replaced fairy tales

20. What does the writer's use of the expression "blazing a trail" (Paragraph 24) tell you about Gareth Gates and Tiger Woods?

They are fastly becoming popular to people

[Turn over for Questions 21, 22 and 23 on *Page six*

Look at Paragraphs 25 to 28.

21. **In your own words** what, according to Maltby, could be the positive outcomes of admiring David Beckham?

    You could follow a good diet or become good at football

22. According to Mark Griffiths:

    (a) how can idols form a healthy part of people's lives?

    Answer in your own words.

    They can influence people to go on diets and stay healthy/fit

    (b) why have pop stars and film stars replaced political and religious leaders?
    Tick (✓) the appropriate box.

    They are good looking. ☐
    They are easily recognised. ☐
    They are respected and highly regarded. ✓

Think about the passage as a whole.

23. "DAZZLED BY THE STARS"

    Explain why, in your opinion, this is an **appropriate** title.

    The public is amazed and follow celebrities so it is an appropriate title

[END OF QUESTION PAPER]

FOR OFFICIAL USE

p2
p3
p4
p5
p6

TOTAL MARK

[BLANK PAGE]

2006 Reading | Foundation

[BLANK PAGE]

0860/401

NATIONAL
QUALIFICATIONS
2006

WEDNESDAY, 3 MAY
10.35 AM – 11.25 AM

ENGLISH
STANDARD GRADE
Foundation Level
Reading
Text

Read carefully the passage overleaf. It will help if you read it twice. When you have done so, answer the questions. Use the spaces provided in the Question/Answer booklet.

Ain't no mountain high enough

Scott Cory is only 14 but he's already scaled some of the highest, most dangerous rock-faces in the world. **Deborah Netburn** watches "Spider-Boy" in action in California.

1 As she stands in the valley of Yosemite National Park, northern California, Jennifer Cory stares intently through a high-powered telescope trained at a great wall of forbidding grey granite which juts high above the alpine meadow. Though she may look like a devoted bird-watcher, the dark-haired 38-year-old is actually keeping a close eye on her 14-year-old son, the American rock-climbing sensation Scott Cory, who is scaling the 2,900 ft wall. High above his mother, the sandy-haired boy keeps his body pressed close against the wall as he calmly scans the rock for the next tiny nick to use as a hand or foot hold. He makes his way quickly and methodically up the great wall. When at last he comes to a pitch (a small ledge to use as a resting place) he stops and calmly looks down at the forest landscape a full skyscraper's length below him. "He looks just as comfortable as if he was standing in his own front yard," says his mother.

2 This trip to Yosemite, two hours from the Corys' home just north of San Francisco, is part of Scott's training for two rock-climbing feats he has planned for the summer. This week he will climb El Capitan and Half Dome. Then, in August, Scott and his fellow rock-climber Steve Schneider, 43, will fly to Lima, Peru, where they plan to be the first Americans to climb "Welcome to the Slabs of Koricancha", a 2,000 ft near-vertical route up La Esfinge mountain. What makes this climb particularly difficult, besides the few hand and foot holds, is the high altitude. The base of the route is 14,000 ft. But Scott seems unconcerned. "It looks like a lot of fun," he tells me.

3 Although Scott hasn't entered high school yet, he has all the trappings of a sports superstar: a sponsorship clothing deal that he picked up at the age of seven; his own sports agent (who also represents Anna Kournikova); and a lot of media coverage (he's appeared on TV and in *Sports Illustrated* in America). Thanks to his good looks he is also starting to build a female fanbase: in one web chatroom a teenage girl listed him as one of her three favourite stars along with Orlando Bloom and Johnny Depp.

4 Scott, who started climbing on a family holiday when he was 7, set his first record when he was 11 by becoming the youngest person to climb "The Nose" of El Capitan, one of the world's most famous and difficult climbing routes. One month later he became the youngest person to do the climb in one day. Fellow rock-climbers say they admire the dedication that has kept this 14-year-old in the gym for four days a week, five hours a day for the past seven years.

5 "I think what sets Scotty apart from a lot of kids," says Beth Rodden, 23, a climber who has known Scott since he was seven, "is that he is up for any challenge, and that is really the key to his success."

6 Scott's explanation of what keeps him in the gym instead of in front of a PlayStation is simple and short. "I love it, and it's fun for me."

7 Indeed, away from the rock-face, in a café down the street from the University of California at Berkeley, Scott looks and acts entirely his age.

8 At the café, Scott is joined by his "mom" Jennifer, and his dad, Jim.

9 Scott orders a pizza, but when it comes he sends it back because the chef has forgotten to hold the anchovies. To tide him over the waitress brings a small leek and onion tart.

10 Scott eyes the tart suspiciously.

11 "Try it," says his mother.

Scott Cory climbing in Red Rocks, Nevada

12 "You try it, Dad," says Scott, moving the plate closer to his father.

13 An hour later he is back in his element at the Touchstone rock-climbing gym at Mission Cliffs in San Francisco. Gyms like these are becoming increasingly popular in the United States; in the early 1990s there were around five, today there are over 500. Scott bounds through the glass doors, nods hello to a man working at the front desk, and steps into a harness. He clips on a little satchel containing powdery chalk to keep his hands dry, and pulls on a tiny pair of rock-climbing shoes.

14 "Scott usually wears a size nine but those shoes are six and a half," observes his father. "He crams his toes in there so he can feel every little thing when he is climbing the wall."

15 Within ten minutes Scott is moving swiftly up the artificial rock-face. The press has nicknamed him "Spider-Boy" because of his technique, though he says nobody calls him that in real life. But the nickname is good—the way he holds his body parallel to the wall, the way he makes full use of the span of his arms and legs, the trail of rope he leaves behind him as he climbs. In the gym, where he is able to study the routes from the ground, his climbing is more graceful than it is on the mountain.

16 Scott is still unsure what sort of future he will have in rock-climbing.

17 "I think he would love to see himself climbing for a living, but it just isn't a big enough sport," says his mother. "The professional climbers he knows just get by on a measly existence, but he hasn't even entered high school yet, so we have to see what happens. He could decide tomorrow that he doesn't like it anymore. Although I don't think anyone imagines that will happen."

18 Back on the wall Scott works on the final section of the hardest route. Grasping the small rubber holds he swiftly moves upwards. Below, his friends in the gym cheer for him, but just as he reaches the top his hand slips and he is left dangling in the air.

19 Scott has been here three hours already, and he has tried this particular route at least five times. His parents are ready to leave but Scott won't hear of it. He isn't going anywhere until he gets it right.

Adapted from the
Sunday Telegraph Magazine

[*END OF PASSAGE*]

[BLANK PAGE]

Official SQA Past Papers: Foundation English 2006

FOR OFFICIAL USE

F

Total Mark

0860/402

NATIONAL QUALIFICATIONS 2006

WEDNESDAY, 3 MAY 10.35 AM – 11.25 AM

ENGLISH STANDARD GRADE Foundation Level Reading Questions

Fill in these boxes and read what is printed below.

Full name of centre

Town

Forename(s)

Surname

Date of birth
Day Month Year

Scottish candidate number

Number of seat

NB Before leaving the examination room you must give this booklet to the invigilator. If you do not, you may lose all the marks for this paper.

SCOTTISH QUALIFICATIONS AUTHORITY

SA 0860/401 6/32070

QUESTIONS

Write your answers in the spaces provided.

Look at Paragraph 1.

1. Where **exactly** in northern California is Jennifer Cory as she watches her son climb?

   _____

2. Write down the expression which suggests that Jennifer is concentrating very hard on what she is doing.

   _____

3. "Though she may look like a devoted bird-watcher . . ."

   Give a reason why Jennifer could be mistaken for a bird-watcher.

   _____

4. ". . . a great wall of forbidding grey granite . . ."

   What impression do we get of the mountain from this description?

   _____

5. **Write down three separate words** the writer uses in Paragraph 1 to suggest Scott Cory is a good climber.

   [_____]   [_____]   [_____]

6. ". . . **a full skyscraper's length below him**"

   Explain fully why the writer uses this expression here.

   _____
   _____

Look at Paragraph 2.

7. "'It looks like a lot of fun,' he tells me."

    Give **two** reasons why the reader might find Scott's statement surprising.

    (i) _____

    (ii) _____

Look at Paragraph 3.

8. (a) Give **three** pieces of evidence that show Scott ". . . has all the trappings of a sports superstar".

    _____

    _____

    (b) Why are the words *Sports Illustrated* in italics?

    _____

Look at Paragraph 4.

9. What were the first **two** climbing records which Scott set?

    (i) _____

    (ii) _____

10. Write down **one word** which **sums up** Scott's attitude to training.

[Turn over

Look at Paragraphs 7 to 12.

11. Why does the writer put inverted commas around "mom"?

    _____

12. In the café, how does Scott behave like a typical teenager?

    _____

    _____

Look at Paragraphs 13 and 14.

13. What evidence does the writer give to show that rock climbing gyms ". . . are becoming increasingly popular" (Paragraph 13)?

    _____

14. **Write down an expression** from Paragraph 13 which suggests Scott is eager to begin training.

    _____

15. (a) Why does Scott have to "cram" his toes into his rock-climbing shoes?

    _____

    (b) What does he gain from doing this?

    _____

Look at Paragraph 15.

16. (*a*) "The press has nicknamed him Spider-Boy . . ."

Tick (✓) the **three best** reasons why, **according to the passage**, this is a good nickname.

His rope looks like a spider's thread. ☐

He is very young. ☐

He looks like a character from a comic. ☐

He uses his arms and legs at full stretch. ☐

He holds his body at the same angle as the wall. ☐

He is climbing indoors. ☐

(*b*) Which expression, **used later in the passage**, reminds the reader of this comparison with a spider?

_____

Look at Paragraphs 16 and 17.

17. **Write down an expression** which suggests that some professional climbers do not make much money from the sport.

_____

Look at Paragraphs 18 and 19.

18. What **two** pieces of evidence show that Scott does not like to give up on a climb?

_____

_____

[Turn over for Question 19 on Page six

Think about the passage as a whole.

19. (a) What impression do you, as a reader, get of Scott Cory?

(b) Give **two** pieces of evidence from the passage to support your answer.

[END OF QUESTION PAPER]

FOR OFFICIAL USE

p2	
p3	
p4	
p5	
p6	
TOTAL MARK	

[0860/402]

Page seven

[BLANK PAGE]

2006 Reading | General

0860/403

NATIONAL
QUALIFICATIONS
2006

WEDNESDAY, 3 MAY
1.00 PM – 1.50 PM

ENGLISH
STANDARD GRADE
General Level
Reading
Text

Read carefully the passage overleaf. It will help if you read it twice. When you have done so, answer the questions. Use the spaces provided in the Question/Answer booklet.

In this extract from a novel set in a secondary school, the narrator, John, is sitting in his Maths class. Gloria (nicknamed Glory Hallelujah) is another pupil in the same class.

1   I am sitting in school, in Maths, with a piece of paper in my hand. No, it is not my algebra homework. It is not a quiz that I have finished and am waiting to hand in to Mrs Moonface. The piece of paper in my hand has nothing at all to do with Mathematics. Nor does it have to do with any school subject. Nor is it really a piece of paper at all.

2   It is really my fate, masquerading as paper.

3   I am sitting next to Glory Hallelujah and I am waiting for a break in the action. Mrs Moonface is at the front of the room, going on about integers. I am not hearing a single thing that she is saying. She could stop lecturing about integers and start doing a cancan kick or singing a rap song and I would not notice.

4   She could call on me and ask me any question on earth, and I would not be able to answer.

5   But luckily, she does not call on me. She has a piece of chalk in her right hand. She is waving it around like a dagger as she spews algebra gibberish at a hundred miles a minute.

6   I hear nothing. Algebra does not have the power to penetrate my feverish isolation.

7   You see, I am preparing to ask Glory Hallelujah out on a date.

8   I am on an island, even though I am sitting at my desk surrounded by my classmates.

9   I am on Torture Island.

10 There are no trees on Torture Island—no huts, no hills, no beaches. There is only doubt.

11 Gloria will laugh at me. That thought is my lonely and tormenting company here on Torture Island. The exact timing and nature of her laughter are open to endless speculation.

12 She may not take me seriously. Her response may be "Oh, John, do you exist? Are you here on earth with me? I wasn't aware we were sharing the same universe."

13 Or she may be even more sarcastic. "John, I would love to go on a date with you, but I'm afraid I have to change my cat's litter box that night ."

14 So, as you can see, Torture Island is not exactly a beach resort. I am not having much fun here. I am ready to seize my moment and leave Torture Island forever.

15 In registration, I ripped a piece of paper from my yellow notepad. My black ball-point pen shook slightly in my trembling right hand as I wrote out the fateful question: "Gloria, will you go out with me this Friday?" Beneath that monumental question, I drew two boxes. One box was conspicuously large. I labelled it the YES box. The second box was tiny. I labelled it the NO box.

16 And that is the yellow piece of paper I have folded up into a square and am holding in my damp hand as I wait here on Torture Island for Mrs Moonface to turn towards the blackboard and give me the opportunity I need.

17 I cannot approach Glory Hallelujah after class because she is always surrounded by her friends. I cannot wait and pass the note to her later in the week because she may make plans to go out with one of her girlfriends. No, it is very evident to me that today is the day, and that I must pass the note before this period ends or forever live a coward.

18 There are only ten minutes left in Maths and Mrs Moonface seems to have no intention of recording her algebraic observations for posterity. Perhaps the piece of yellow chalk in her hand is just a prop. It is possible that the previous night she hurt her wrist in an arm-wrestling competition and can no longer write. It is also possible that she has forgotten all about her pupils and believes that she is playing a part in a Hollywood movie.

19 There are only seven minutes left in Maths. I attempt to turn Mrs Moonface towards the blackboard by telekinesis. The atoms of her body prove remarkably resistant to my telepathic powers.

20 There are six minutes left. Now there are five.

21 Mrs Moonface, for Pete's sake, write something on the blackboard! That is what Mathematics teachers do! Write down axioms, simplify equations, draw rectangles, measure angles, even, if you must, sketch the sneering razor-toothed face of Algebra itself. WRITE ANYTHING!

22 Suddenly Mrs Moonface stops lecturing.

23 Her right hand, holding the chalk, rises.

24 Then her hips begin to pivot.

25 This all unfolds in very slow motion. The sheer importance of the moment slows the action way, way down.

26 The pivoting of Mrs Moonface's hips causes a corresponding rotation in the plane of her shoulders and upper torso.

27 Her neck follows her shoulders, as day follows night.

28 Eventually, the lunar surface of her face is pulled towards the blackboard.

29 She begins to write. I have no idea what she is writing. It could be hieroglyphics and I would not notice. It could be a map to Blackbeard's treasure and I would not care.

30 I am now primed. My heart is thumping against my ribs, one by one, like a hammer pounding out a musical scale on a metal keyboard. Bing. Bang. Bong. Bam. I am breathing so quickly that I cannot breathe, if that makes any sense.

31 I am aware of every single one of my classmates in Maths.

32 Everyone in Maths is now preoccupied. There are only four minutes left in the period. Mrs Moonface is filling up blackboard space at an unprecedented speed, no doubt trying to scrape every last kernel of mathematical knowledge from the corncob of her brain before the bell. My classmates are racing to keep up with her. All around me pens are moving across notebooks at such a rate that ink can barely leak out and affix itself to paper.

33 My moment is at hand! The great clapper in the bell of fate clangs for me! *Ka-wang! Ka-wang!*

34 My right hand rises and begins to move sideways, very slowly, like a submarine, travelling at sub-desk depth to avoid teacher radar.

35 My right index finger makes contact with the sacred warm left wrist of Glory Hallelujah!

36 She looks down to see who is touching her at sub-desk depth. Spots my hand, with its precious yellow note.

37 Gloria understands instantly.

38 The exchange of the covert note is completed in a nanoinstant. Mrs Moonface and the rest of our Maths class have no idea that anything momentous has taken place.

39 I reverse the speed and direction of my right hand, and it returns safely to port.

40 Gloria has transferred my note to her lap and has moved her right elbow to block anyone on that side of her from seeing. The desk itself provides added shielding.

41 In the clever safe haven that she has created, she unfolds my note. Reads it.

42 She does not need to speak. She does not need to check the YES or NO boxes on my note. If she merely blinks, I will understand. If she wrinkles her nose, the import of her nose wrinkle will not be lost on me. In fact, so total is my concentration in that moment of grand suspense I am absolutely positive that there is nothing that Glory Hallelujah can do, no reaction that she can give off, that I will not immediately and fully understand.

43 I would stake my life on it.

44 But what she does do is this. She folds my note back up. Without looking at me—without even an eye blink or a nose wrinkle—she raises it to her lips. For one wild instant I think that she is going to kiss it.

45 Her pearly teeth part.

46 She eats my note.

Adapted from the novel *You Dont Know Me* By David Klass

[END OF PASSAGE]

FOR OFFICIAL USE

G

Total Mark

0860/404

NATIONAL QUALIFICATIONS 2006

WEDNESDAY, 3 MAY 1.00 PM – 1.50 PM

ENGLISH STANDARD GRADE General Level Reading Questions

Fill in these boxes and read what is printed below.

Full name of centre

Town

Forename(s)

Surname

Date of birth
Day Month Year

Scottish candidate number

Number of seat

NB Before leaving the examination room you must give this booklet to the invigilator. If you do not, you may lose all the marks for this paper.

SCOTTISH QUALIFICATIONS AUTHORITY

SA 0860/401 6/67270

QUESTIONS

Write your answers in the spaces provided.

Look at Paragraphs 1 to 4.

1. (*a*) Who is Mrs Moonface?

   _____

   (*b*) Why do you think John gives her the nickname "Mrs Moonface"?

   _____
   _____

2. "It is really my fate, masquerading as paper."

   Why does the writer place this sentence in a paragraph of its own?

   _____
   _____

3. "Mrs Moonface is at the front of the room, going on about integers."

   What does the expression "going on" suggest about John's attitude to what Mrs Moonface is saying?

   _____

Look at Paragraphs 5 to 10.

4. How does the writer make Mrs Moonface's behaviour seem threatening?

   _____
   _____

5. "... spews algebra gibberish at a hundred miles a minute..." (Paragraph 5)

Explain in your own words what the writer's word choice in this expression suggests about what John thinks of:

(i) **what** she is saying;

_____

_____

(ii) **how** she says it.

_____

_____

6. "... I am preparing to ask Glory Hallelujah out on a date." (Paragraph 7)

Why do you think the writer waits until this point to reveal what John is planning to do?

_____

_____

7. "I am on Torture Island." (Paragraph 9)

(a) **Explain fully in your own words** what the narrator means by this.

_____

_____

(b) Write down an expression from later in the passage which contains a similar idea.

[Turn over

8. Explain how the writer emphasises the bleakness of "Torture Island".

Look at Paragraphs 11 to 14.

9. (*a*) **Write down an example** of the writer's use of humour in these paragraphs.

(*b*) Explain why your chosen example is funny.

Look at Paragraphs 15 to 17.

10. **Write down three** pieces of evidence that suggest the narrator's nervousness at this point in the story.

11. Quote **two** separate words used by the writer to suggest the importance of what John is asking Gloria.

12. "One box was conspicuously large . . . The second box was tiny." (Paragraph 15)

Why do you think John makes the boxes different sizes?

Page four

[0860/404]

13. **In your own words**, give a reason why John must make his approach to Gloria during Maths.

   _____

   _____

Look at Paragraphs 18 to 21.

14. How does the writer suggest the mood of increasing tension at this point in the passage?

   _____

   _____

15. "WRITE ANYTHING!" (Paragraph 21)

   Why are these words written in capital letters?

   _____

   _____

Look at Paragraphs 22 to 33

16. (a) Identify any **one** technique used by the writer in this section to suggest John's growing excitement.

   _____

   (b) Explain **how** it does so.

   _____

   _____

[Turn over for Questions 17 to 20 on *Page six*

Look at Paragraphs 34 to 46.

17. Give **three** reasons why Mrs Moonface is unaware of the note being passed.

   _____
   _____
   _____

18. Why does John feel the "YES" or "NO" boxes on his note are now irrelevant?

   _____
   _____

19. How does the final paragraph provide an effective end to the passage?

   _____
   _____

Now look at the passage as a whole.

20. How realistic do you find the writer's description of this classroom incident? Give reasons for your opinion.

   _____
   _____
   _____

[END OF QUESTION PAPER]

FOR OFFICIAL USE

p2
p3
p4
p5
p6
TOTAL MARK

[0860/404] *Page seven*

[BLANK PAGE]

2007 Reading | Foundation

[BLANK PAGE]

0860/401

NATIONAL
QUALIFICATIONS
2007

TUESDAY, 1 MAY
10.35 AM – 11.25 AM

ENGLISH
STANDARD GRADE
Foundation Level
Reading
Text

Read carefully the passage overleaf. It will help if you read it twice. When you have done so, answer the questions. Use the spaces provided in the Question/Answer booklet.

Why dumped dog is such a lucky hound

No one wanted greyhound Pal after he was abandoned for not being fast enough on the track—until an animal trainer was asked to find a dog to star in a film. DAVID WIGG tells how the renamed Celt so nearly lost out again—before finding a new home and some much-needed love.

1 As Celt the greyhound comes bounding over to me on green fields overlooking the picturesque fields of Kent, he obviously knows he is a dog in a million. Once abandoned, he is now the star of a heartwarming film.

2 Celt, with his golden fawn markings, is one of many unwanted greyhounds in Britain that are dumped if they don't come up to racing standards.

3 He had ended up being abandoned at a greyhound rescue centre. As the weeks went by, no one came to adopt Celt as a family pet but then something even more exciting happened to him.

4 Animal handler Sue Potter had been asked to find an appealing greyhound to star in the film entitled "The Mighty Celt", a touching story about a boy and his love and devotion for a dog he desperately wants to own.

5 Sue had the almost impossible task of choosing one greyhound from more than 100 at the kennels.

6 But when she saw Celt, or Pal, as he was then known, Sue immediately knew he was the one she could train for the film. So what was so special about Celt?

7 "His colouring was perfect, he had to be fawn with some white markings," says Sue. "He also had to be obedient and compatible with people and other animals.

8 "I tested his reaction to sound and that was fine. There couldn't be anything wrong with him—he had to be an entire dog."

9 Sue trained Celt for two weeks at her home in the north of England, in preparation for his starring role. Celt then spent eight weeks filming in Northern Ireland with the cast and crew.

10 From all accounts, Celt excelled himself on set and everyone fell in love with him, but after the filming there was one big question remaining—what was to become of Celt? After all the attention he had received, it didn't seem right that he should go back to being alone and unwanted once again at the kennels, but Sue felt she couldn't keep him as she already owned five dogs.

11 Urgent inquiries were made among the crew and cast but it seemed no one was able to take him on from the film set where he had been thoroughly pampered.

12 On hearing of the young dog's plight, Kent landowner and farmer Philip Daubeny came to the rescue. Philip is chairman of the London-based charity Dogs Trust, which cares for more than 12,500 strays each year.

13 He had recently lost his own pet greyhound Tocki, another rescued dog. To everyone's relief he agreed to adopt Celt and take him to his lovely country home surrounded by 500 acres of open

hills and farmland near Maidstone. Here Celt now enjoys long walks and romps with Philip's other pets—corgis Dusty and Yehudi and five cats.

14 With Celt looking a picture of contentment, fully spread out in an armchair, Philip recalls: "The first I heard of him was through a vet in Northern Ireland called Rose McIlrath.

15 "One of her friends, Claire Millar, was working as a teacher with the children on the film. When it turned out that no real provision had been made for what was going to happen to Celt, Claire asked Rose if she had any ideas.

16 "Rose immediately thought of me because I had recently lost Tocki, who had been with me for seven years." Philip felt there was one important question that had to be asked before he agreed to take on Celt.

17 How did the greyhound get on with cats? "I was concerned because, on the whole, greyhounds are well known for chasing small furry animals, either cats or small dogs, often mistaking them for the hare on the track. I didn't want some terrible tragedy to happen with my five cats.

18 "I was assured that, after coming back to this country, Celt had been living with cats in a temporary home and I was assured of his character and that he would make a wonderful pet."

19 It was then arranged for Celt to be shipped over to the Dogs Trust Kenilworth Rehoming Centre, in Warwickshire. There he was thoroughly checked over.

20 Celt was driven down in an animal ambulance from Warwickshire to his new home in Kent in July last year.

21 "He was slightly anxious but he quickly settled down. We let him out in the field to meet the other dogs. He got on immediately with them and was keener to play with them than they were with him. He fitted in very easily and quickly, and made himself at home by sitting on every chair he could.

22 "He also wanted to jump on the beds as well, but there isn't much room to sleep if you have a greyhound on board. People think greyhounds need a lot of exercise but, actually, there's nothing they like more than curling up in an armchair and watching television."

23 I couldn't help wondering if, having been pampered on set, Celt acted like a film star. The response was laughter as Philip recalls: "He was very active and bursting with energy.

24 "At first, he rushed around as if he were on a greyhound track but, otherwise, he was among the more likeable and less affected film stars.

25 "Most affectionate, very beautiful and a genuine, kind, loving dog, that is marvellous with children."

26 Dog trainer Sue Potter adds: "I didn't want to take Celt back to the kennels because he had had a life of luxury on the film. I asked around if anyone would like to adopt him. The young boy in the film, Tyrone, fancied having him, but his father was moving house so he said no.

27 "I wanted him to go to a nice home—and he couldn't have gone to a better one. He was very lucky because he really has fallen on his feet."

Adapted from an article by David Wigg

[END OF PASSAGE]

[BLANK PAGE]

Official SQA Past Papers: Foundation English 2007

FOR OFFICIAL USE

F

Total Mark

0860/402

NATIONAL QUALIFICATIONS 2007

TUESDAY, 1 MAY 10.35 AM – 11.25 AM

ENGLISH
STANDARD GRADE
Foundation Level
Reading
Questions

Fill in these boxes and read what is printed below.

Full name of centre

Town

Forename(s)

Surname

Date of birth
Day Month Year

Scottish candidate number

Number of seat

NB Before leaving the examination room you must give this booklet to the invigilator. If you do not, you may lose all the marks for this paper.

SA 0860/402 6/38070

SCOTTISH QUALIFICATIONS AUTHORITY

QUESTIONS

Write your answers in the spaces provided.

Look at the Introduction and Paragraphs 1 to 3.

1. (a) Write down **one** word from Paragraph 1 which suggests that Celt the greyhound is a fit and healthy dog.

   [   ]

   (b) Write down an expression from Paragraph 1 which suggests that this might not always have been the case.

   [   ]

2. "... don't come up to racing standards." (Paragraph 2)

   Write down an expression from the introduction to the passage which contains a similar idea.

   _____

Look at Paragraphs 4 and 5.

3. "... a touching story about a boy and his love and devotion for a dog" (Paragraph 4)

   Tick (✓) the box beside the best definition of "touching" as it is used in this sentence.

exciting	
true	
fictional	
moving	

4. "... the almost impossible task ..." (Paragraph 5)

Why was Sue Potter's task so difficult?

_____

Look at Paragraphs 6 to 8.

5. Write down any **three** qualities Celt needed to have if he was to become a film star.

_____

_____

_____

Look at Paragraphs 9 to 11.

6. Tick (✓) the appropriate box to show whether the following statements are **True**, **False**, or **Cannot tell from the passage**.

	True	False	Cannot Tell
Sue trained Celt in Northern Ireland.			
Celt spent more time being filmed than being trained.			
Celt did well on the film set.			
Sue Potter owns two cats.			

7. Why does the writer use a **dash (—)** in the first sentence of Paragraph 10?

_____

8. Write down an expression which suggests that Celt had been very well cared for during filming.

_____

[Turn over

Look at Paragraphs 12 to 14.

9. Give **three** reasons why Philip Daubeny was a suitable person to rescue Celt.

Look at Paragraphs 15 to 18.

10. "..., Claire Millar, was working as a teacher with the children on the film." (Paragraph 15)

    Why do you think the children on the film needed a teacher?

11. (a) Why was Philip Daubeny concerned for the safety of his cats?

    (b) "I didn't want some terrible tragedy to happen with my five cats." (Paragraph 17)

    Identify **two** techniques used in this sentence to emphasise his concern.

    (c) Do you think "tragedy" is a good word to use here? Give a reason.

12. "... had been living with cats in a temporary home ..." (Paragraph 18)

Tick (✓) the box beside the best definition of "temporary" as it is used in this sentence.

long-lasting	
short-term	
animal	
caring	

Look at Paragraphs 19 to 22.

13. Give **two** pieces of evidence which show how Celt "fitted in very easily". (Paragraph 21)

_____

_____

14. What might some people find surprising about greyhounds?

_____

_____

Look at Paragraphs 23 to 27.

15. How does the structure of the sentence in Paragraph 25 emphasise Celt's good points?

_____

16. Why was the young boy in the film unable to adopt Celt?

_____

[*Turn over for Questions 17 to 19 on Page six*]

17. In what way had Celt "fallen on his feet" (Paragraph 27)?

_____

_____

Think about the passage as a whole.

18. Who do you think this passage is written for? Tick (✓) **one** box.

Film students	
Vets	
General readers	
Dog breeders	

19. "Why dumped dog is such a lucky hound"

Identify **two** techniques which help to make this a good title.

_____

_____

[END OF QUESTION PAPER]

FOR OFFICIAL USE

p2	
p3	
p4	
p5	
p6	
TOTAL MARK	

[BLANK PAGE]

0860/403

NATIONAL
QUALIFICATIONS
2007

TUESDAY, 1 MAY
1.00 PM – 1.50 PM

ENGLISH
STANDARD GRADE
General Level
Reading
Text

Read carefully the passage overleaf. It will help if you read it twice. When you have done so, answer the questions. Use the spaces provided in the Question/Answer booklet.

Biker Boys and Girls

There is only one "wall of death" doing the rounds at British fairs today. But a new generation of daredevil riders is intent on keeping the show on (or rather, off) the road.

1   Last year Kerri Cameron, aged 19 and a little bored with her job as a horse-riding instructor, was looking up job vacancies on the internet. Puzzled, she turned to her mother and said, "Mum, what's a wall of death?"

2   Her mother, Denise, a health worker who has always had a horror of motorcycles, told her that walls of death were places where people rode motorbikes round the insides of a 20 ft-high wooden drum and tried not to fall off and get killed. "Gosh," said Kerri, "that sounds fun."

3   She picked up her mobile, phoned the number mentioned on the internet and then arranged to see Ken Fox, owner of the wall of death. Ken Fox didn't ask about her school qualifications, only if she wanted a ride on the back of his bike around the wall. Yes, she said.

4   Ken Fox revved up the demonstration bike and spun it on to the 45-degree wooden apron that bridges the ground and the perpendicular wall and then took it three or four times around the lower bits of the wall itself just to see if she could cope. Then he went round with Kerri sitting on the handlebars. She passed that test, too. She thought it was fantastic. Unbelievable. The best!

5   A year later Kerri is doing 20 shows a day, driving a skeletal aluminium go-kart around Ken Fox's wall of death to within six inches of the safety wire at the top—the wire that's there to prevent the machines sailing off into the crowd. "It's much more fun than helping kids on horses," she says, giggling nervously and brushing a strand of blonde hair back behind her ear. "The only thing I really miss about home is flush toilets."

6   Ken Fox and his wife Julie, their sons, Luke and Alex, and their troupe of Kerri, a new girl rider called Emma Starr, a man who prefers to be known just as Philip, and a wall-of-death enthusiast of an accountant named Neil Calladine, now operate the last wall of death in business in Britain. Calladine is the wall's "spieler", stalking the front of the attraction with a microphone, promising thrills and excitement as Ken and Luke Fox sit on their bikes, creating the roaring throttle noises of impending danger. Later, Luke and his father dip and zig-zag their bikes across each other, spinning round the drum every four seconds, as the holiday crowds peer tentatively down over the safety wire and then, in the traditional way, shower coins into the ring after being told that wall-of-death riders can never get insurance. Each show lasts 20 minutes; at one stage four riders are zipping up, down and all around.

7   In the 1930s and 1940s there were almost 30 walls of death at seaside resorts and fairgrounds around the country, often competing side-by-side in fairgrounds; now there are four left. One is in a steam museum in Derbyshire, another is the hobby/toy of a Cornish builder, and a third is owned by a 54-year-old agricultural engineer who "has done everything in motorcycles except ridden a wall of death". That wall's old owner, Graham Cripsey, of the Cripsey fairground family, is coming down from Skegness to teach him how to ride it.

8   Only Ken Fox and his band, together with pet dog Freebie, two ferrets and two cockatiels, tour in the traditional way, squelching out of their winter quarters from behind the Cambridgeshire hedgerows just before Easter and heading in convoy for the first of the 6,000 miles they will complete by the end of October. Ken is lucky that Julie can drive one of the trucks, change the 2 ft-high tyres, make sure Alex does his school lessons on his laptop, cook, make sandwiches and dish out the £2 tickets. She, too, loves the travelling life. "When you think I used to be a dental nurse," she says, her eyes misting a little.

9   She also helped her husband build his wall of death. "My old wall was wearing out," he says, "so I bought a 200 ft section of very long,

very straight, Oregon pine that cost £70,000 (Oregon pine, one of the tallest trees in the world, is used for all walls of death because of the straightness of its grain and the lack of knot in its timber). I got the planks cut in a milling yard. I went to a boatyard where they built submarines. The place was so big we could have built 50 walls of death."

10   The motorbikes used for shows are Indian Scouts made in the 1920s by the Hendee Motorcycle Company of Springfield, Massachusetts, deliberately engineered for easy balance with all the controls on the left, so Chicago cops could use their right hands for drawing their revolvers and shooting at Al Capone-style gangsters. This means the bikes are perfect for tricks. Take your hand off the throttle of a modern motorbike and it slips back to idling mode, thus losing the power that keeps the bike on the wall. Take your hand off the throttle of an Indian Scout, and the revs stay as they are—which means that you can zoom round and round the wall of death, arms in the air, to your heart's content.

11   The first wall of death is said by Graham Cripsey to have come to Britain from America in 1928 with others close on its heels. His grandfather, Walter, and father, Roy, trained lions to ride in the sidecars, as did the famous George "Tornado" Smith at Southend's Kursaal fairground. The Cripseys also developed a technique of being towed round behind the Indian Scouts on roller skates. "If you were competing side by side in a fairground, you always had to have one stunt better than the other," explains Graham. Smith also kept a skeleton in a sidecar which, with a flick on a control, would suddenly sit bolt upright. And Ricky Abrey, 61, who rode with him as "The Black Baron", says Tornado perfected a ride where three riders would cut off their engines at the top of the wall and instantly re-start them again, causing the audience to gasp as 2 ft-long flashes of flame escaped the exhaust pipes.

12   Fun, then, for all the family. "People still love the wall of death," says Ken Fox emphatically. "People like what we put on and get good value for it. If they see it once, they always want to see it again. The problem is finding the people to work on it. There are a lot of soft men around."

13   "Wall of death" is, thankfully, a bit of a misnomer, for there have been no fatal accidents on British walls, though whether that's due to good luck or fear-induced careful preparation is difficult to tell. "I've been knocked off by other riders, the engine's stalled, I've had punctures and I've hit a safety cable," says Ken Fox, pointing at his scars. "Everyone gets falls at some time but we try to be spot-on in our preparations. Before every show we spend a complete day trying to get the machines working perfectly."

14   Luke Fox suffered his first bad fall last year, flicking a safety-cable bolt on one of his "dips" as he zig-zagged his bike up and down. He fell 20 ft, got up and started again, even though he'd severely torn his knee. In a sense, he's got his own good-luck charm. His Indian bike was originally ridden by no less a daredevil than Tornado Smith himself. Luke has also inherited his father's total dedication to the trade and the Fox family wall looks set to last into the immediate future. Indeed, he and Kerri are now a partnership, sharing the long-haul driving and other things, while young Alex, the ferret-fancier, is raring for his first go at the wall.

15   Even Neil Calladine, the spieler, has shed his accountant duties and can indulge his lifelong passion for fairgrounds, though he needs to talk almost non-stop from 2 pm to 10 pm each show day and consumes mountains of throat sweets. "I make sure I go back and see the missus once a month," he says, "and of course I'm there all winter. I suppose I'm one of those fortunate people whose hobby has become his life. I love the freedom of travel, no nine-to-five, just us and the open road."

16   In that he's just like Kerri Cameron, bless her daredevil heart.

Adapted from an article
by John Dodd

[END OF PASSAGE]

[BLANK PAGE]

FOR OFFICIAL USE

G

0860/404

Total Mark

NATIONAL QUALIFICATIONS 2007

TUESDAY, 1 MAY 1.00 PM – 1.50 PM

ENGLISH
STANDARD GRADE
General Level
Reading
Questions

Fill in these boxes and read what is printed below.

Full name of centre

Town

Forename(s)

Surname

Date of birth
Day Month Year

Scottish candidate number

Number of seat

NB Before leaving the examination room you must give this booklet to the invigilator. If you do not, you may lose all the marks for this paper.

SCOTTISH QUALIFICATIONS AUTHORITY

SA 0860/404 6/75170

QUESTIONS

Write your answers in the spaces provided.

Look at Paragraphs 1 to 3.

1. **In your own words**, explain fully why Kerri Cameron was looking up job vacancies on the internet.

2. What is surprising about Kerri's reaction to what her mother tells her about the wall of death?

3. Why do you think Ken Fox was not interested in Kerri's school qualifications?

Look at Paragraphs 4 and 5.

4. How does the writer suggest Kerri's enthusiasm after her test on the bike:

   (a) by word choice?

   (b) by sentence structure?

5. **Using your own words as far as possible**, describe **two** aspects of Kerri's performance which could be described as dangerous.

Look at Paragraph 6.

6. **In your own words**, explain the job of the "spieler".

   _____

7. ". . . shower coins into the ring . . ."

   Give **two** reasons why "shower" is an effective word to use in this context.

   _____

   _____

8. Why do you think members of the audience are told that wall-of-death riders "can never get insurance"?

   _____

9. Explain fully what the expression "zipping up, down and all around" suggests about the riders' performance.

   _____

   _____

Look at Paragraphs 7 to 9.

10. How does the writer illustrate the decline in popularity of walls of death?

    _____

[Turn over

11. "Only Ken Fox and his band . . ." (Paragraph 8)

Write down **one** word from earlier in the passage which contains the same idea as "band".

[_____]

12. Explain fully why you think the writer uses the word "squelching" in Paragraph 8.

_____
_____

13. Look again at the sentence which begins "Ken is lucky . . ." (Paragraph 8).

How does the structure of the **whole** sentence help to reinforce how busy Julie is between Easter and October?

_____
_____

14. Why is Oregon pine so suitable for walls of death?

_____

Look at Paragraph 10.

15. Using your own words as far as possible, explain why the Indian Scout bikes are "perfect for tricks."

_____
_____

[0860/404]   Page four

16. Identify two techniques used by the writer which help to involve the reader in his description of the Indian Scout motorbikes. **Quote evidence** from the paragraph to support your answers.

Technique	Evidence

Look at Paragraphs 11 and 12.

17. Why might the nicknames "Tornado" and "The Black Baron" be suitable for wall-of-death riders?

Tornado

_____

The Black Baron

_____

[Turn over

18. (*a*) Write down **four** things the early wall-of-death riders included in their acts.

2 1 0

(*b*) **In your own words**, give **two** reasons why such things were included in the acts.

2 1 0

Look at Paragraphs 13 to 16.

19. "... is, thankfully, a bit of a misnomer, ..." (Paragraph 13)

(*a*) Tick (✓) the box beside the best definition of "misnomer".

old-fashioned attraction	
risky venture	
successful show	
wrongly applied name	

(*b*) Write down evidence from the passage to support your answer to 19(*a*).

2 1 0

20. Why is the word "dips" (Paragraph 14) in inverted commas?

2 ■ 0

21. Give **three** pieces of evidence to support the writer's statement that "the Fox family wall looks set to last into the immediate future" (Paragraph 14).

_____

_____

_____

22. Show how the final paragraph is an effective conclusion to this article.

_____

_____

[END OF QUESTION PAPER]

FOR OFFICIAL USE

p2	
p3	
p4	
p5	
p6	
p7	
TOTAL MARK	

[BLANK PAGE]

[BLANK PAGE]

2005 Writing | Foundation | General | Credit

[BLANK PAGE]

Official SQA Past Papers: Foundation/General/Credit English 2005

F G C

0860/407

NATIONAL QUALIFICATIONS 2005

WEDNESDAY, 4 MAY 9.00 AM – 10.15 AM

ENGLISH STANDARD GRADE Foundation, General and Credit Levels Writing

Read This First

1. Inside this booklet, there are photographs and words.
   Use them to help you when you are thinking about what to write.
   Look at all the material and think about all the possibilities.

2. There are 23 assignments altogether for you to choose from.

3. Decide which assignment you are going to attempt.
   Choose only **one** and write its number in the margin of your answer book.

4. Pay close attention to what you are asked to write.
   Plan what you are going to write.
   Read and check your work before you hand it in.
   Any changes to your work should be made clearly.

SAB 0860/407 6/70570

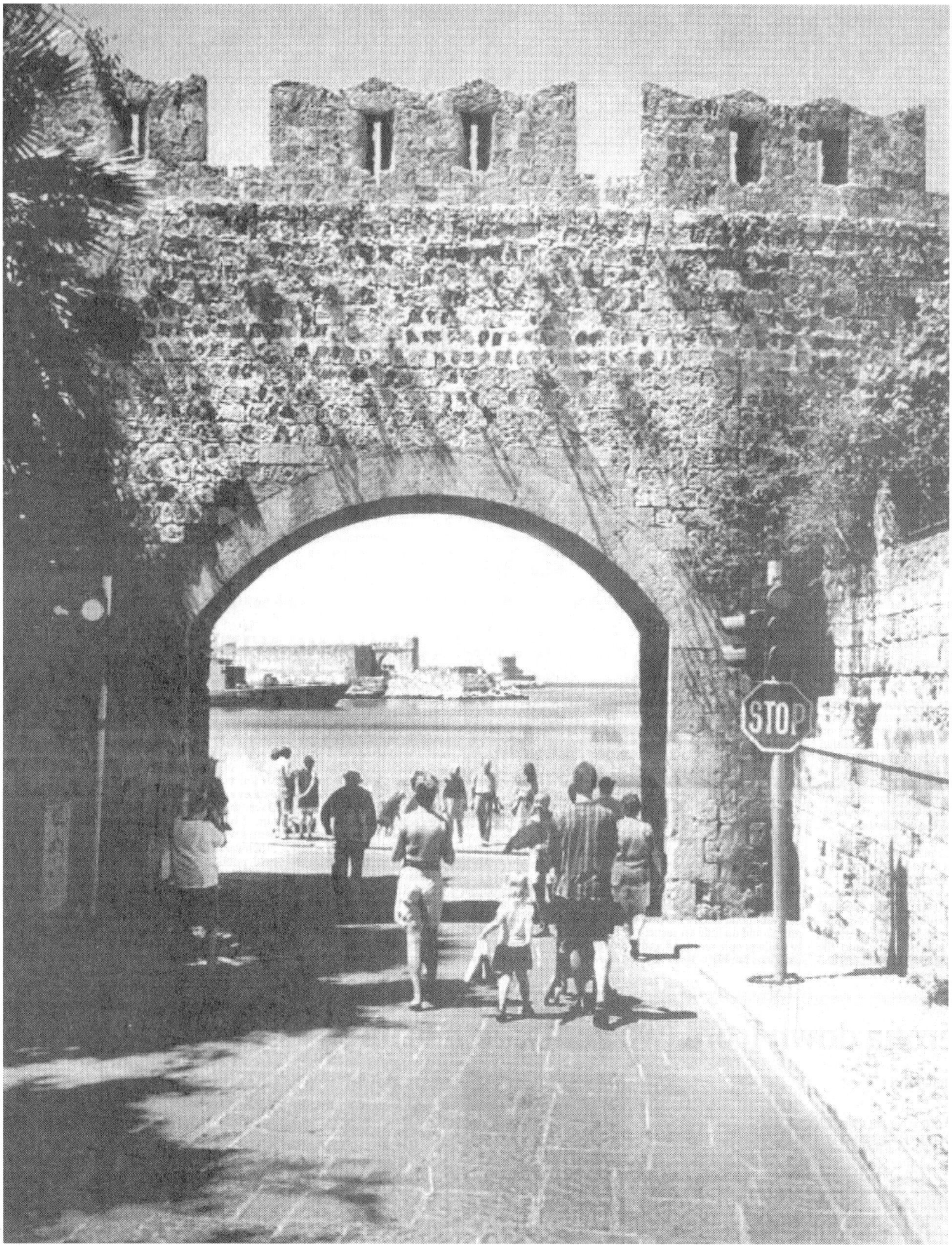
STOP

FIRST   **Look at the picture opposite.
It shows a holiday scene.**

NEXT   Think about holidays.

WHAT YOU HAVE TO WRITE

1. Even the worst holiday can have its funny side.

   Write about your experience of a holiday like this.

   Remember to include your **thoughts and feelings**.

   OR

2. **Write an article for a magazine describing** your favourite holiday resort and outlining its main attractions.

   OR

3. Sun, sea and sand.

   Surely there must be more to a holiday than that?

   Do you agree or disagree? Give your views.

   OR

4. **Write a short story** entitled:

   Going Places.

[Turn over

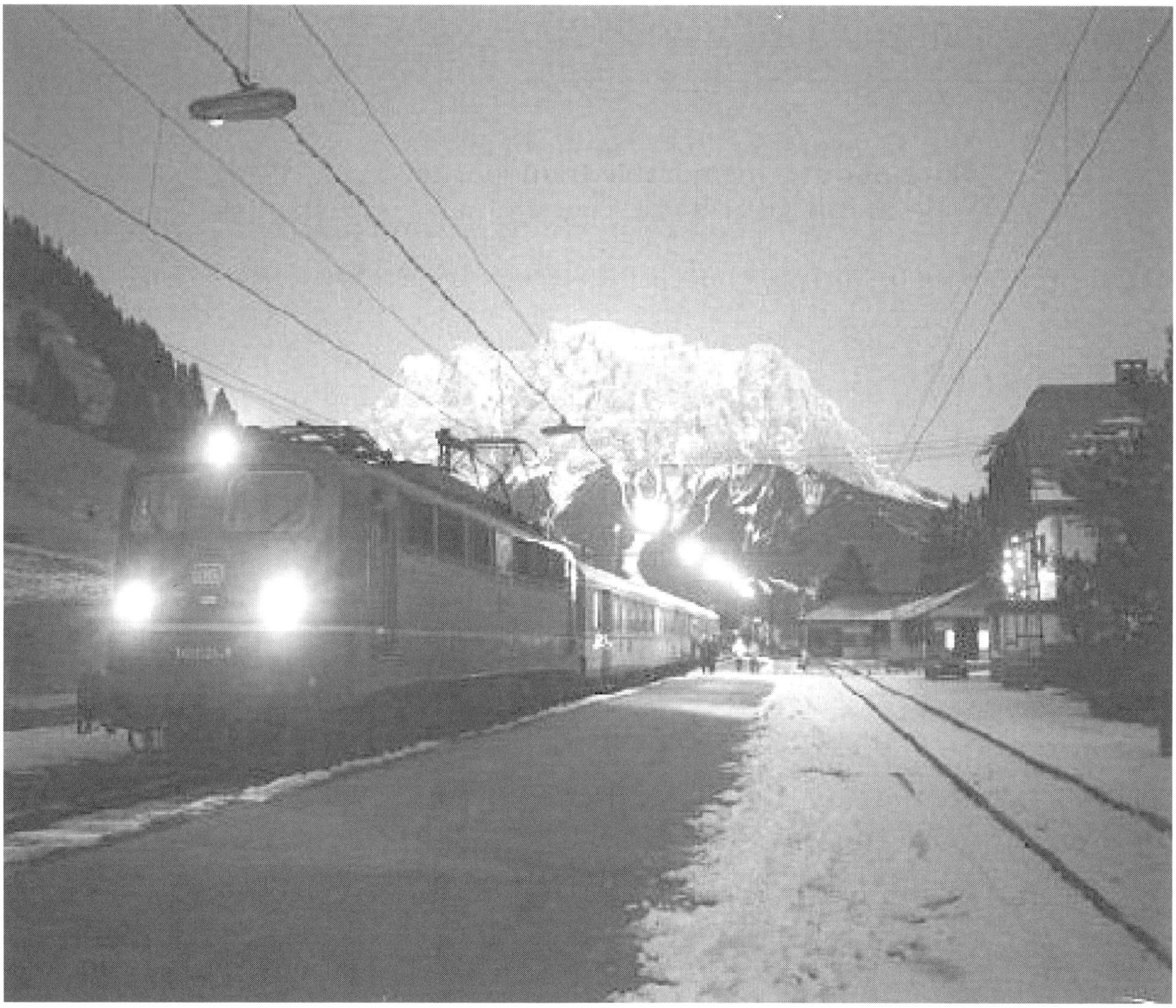

FIRST   **Look at the picture opposite.**
It shows a train in a station at night.

NEXT   Think about journeys by train.

WHAT YOU HAVE TO WRITE

5. **Write about** a memorable train journey.

   Remember to include your **thoughts and feelings.**

   OR

6. Trains and railways are fascinating but can be dangerous.

   Discuss.

   OR

7. **Write a short story** using **ONE** of the following titles:

   Night Train   The Deserted Station   Crossing The Border

   OR

8. Trainspotting—an unusual hobby?

   Do you have a hobby which some people might consider unusual?

   Write about it, making it clear why **you** enjoy it.

[Turn over

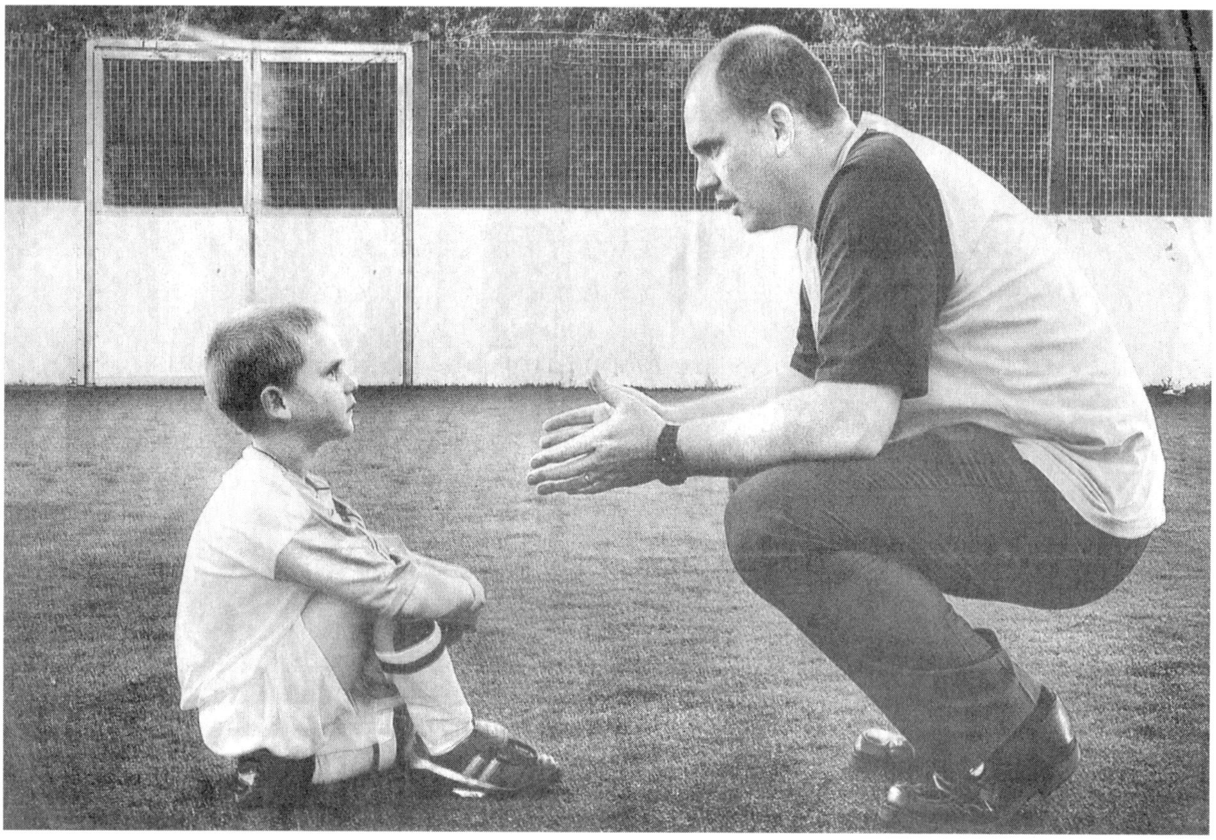

FIRST **Look at the picture opposite.
It shows a father coaching his son.**

NEXT Think about competitive sport.

WHAT YOU HAVE TO WRITE

9. Young people today are under too much pressure to succeed.

   Do you agree or disagree? Give your views.

   OR

10. **Write about** an occasion when you took part in a sporting activity and lost.

    Remember to include your **thoughts and feelings.**

    OR

11. **Write a short story** entitled:

    Determination.

    OR

12. Playing in a team has much more to offer than competing as an individual.

    Do you agree or disagree? Give your views.

[Turn over

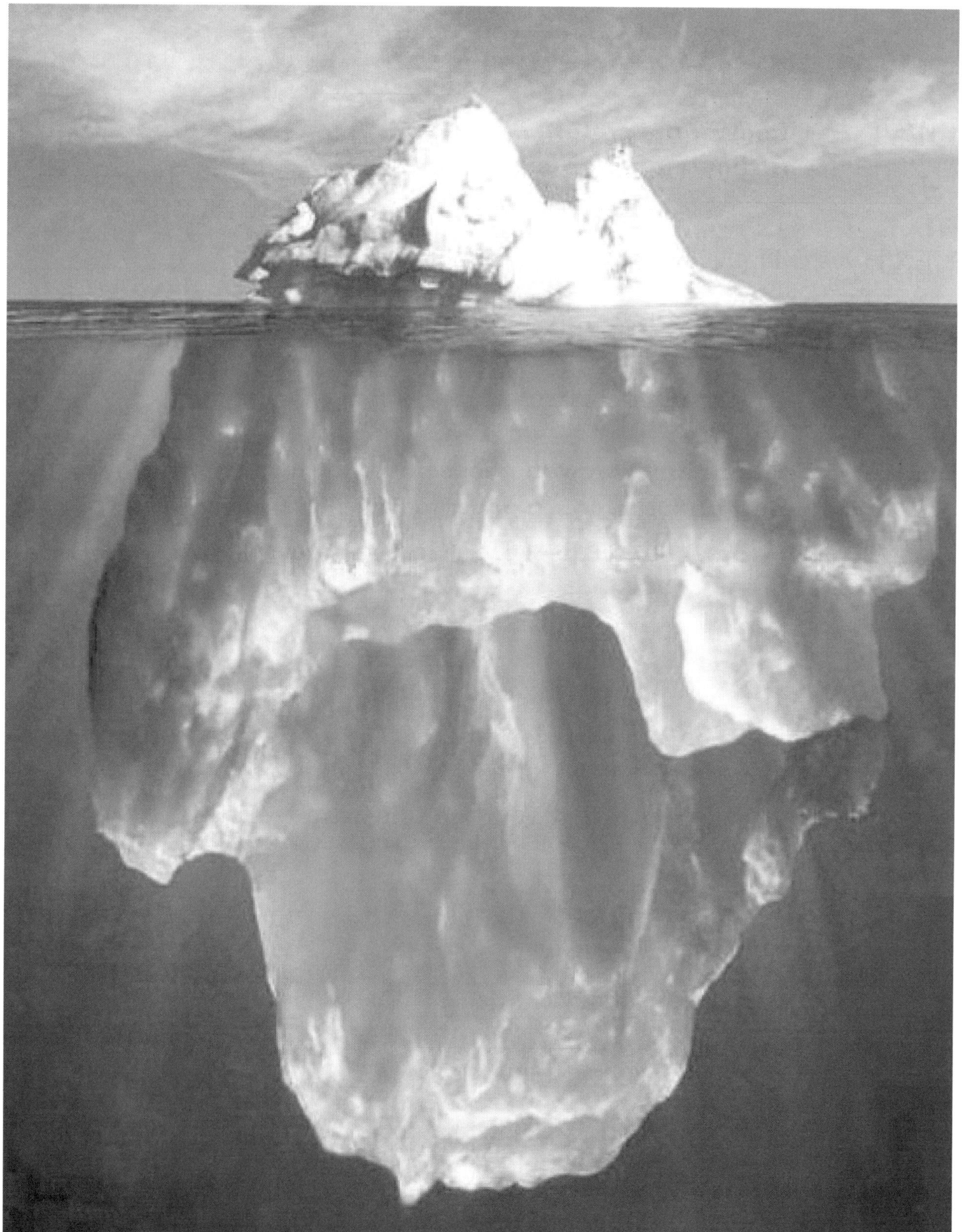

FIRST **Look at the picture opposite.
It shows an iceberg.**

NEXT Think about the beauty and danger of icebergs.

WHAT YOU HAVE TO WRITE

13. **Write in any way you choose** using the picture opposite as your inspiration.

    OR

14. **Write a newspaper article** using the headline:

    Ship Strikes Iceberg!

    OR

15. Global warming will end us if we do not end it.

    Do you agree or disagree? Give your views.

    OR

16. **Write a short story** using **ONE** of the following titles:

    Iceworld   Hidden Depths

[Turn over

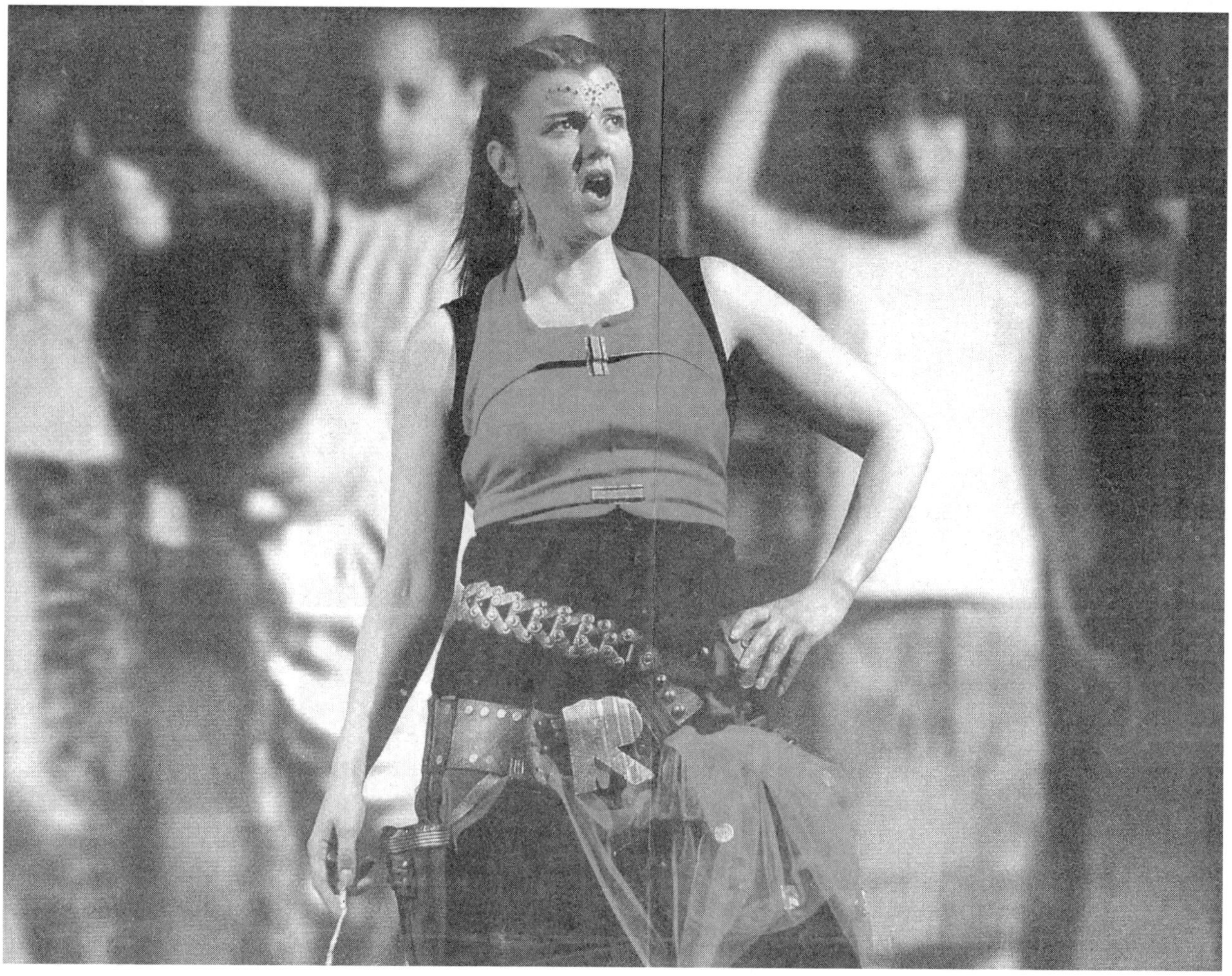

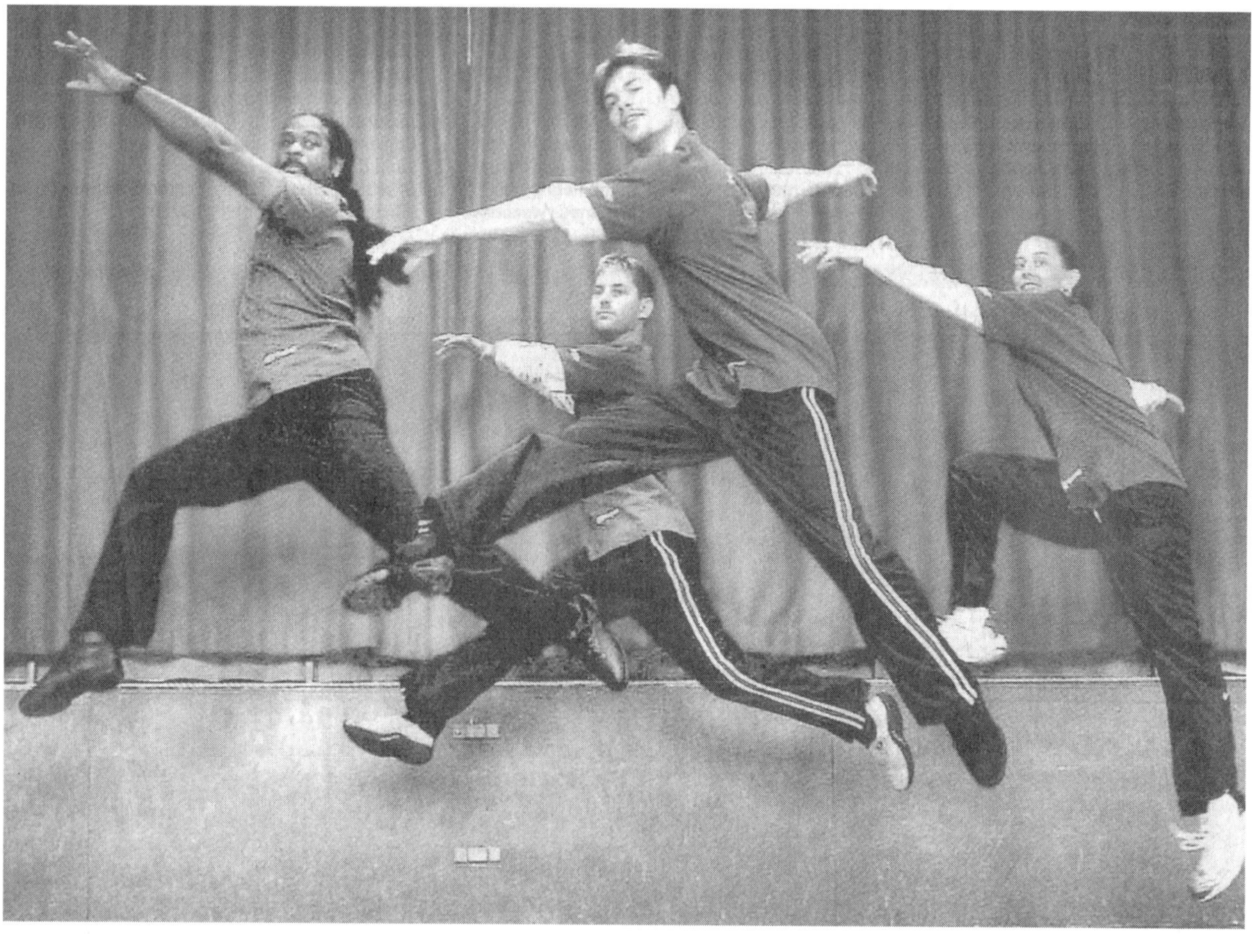

FIRST **Look at the pictures opposite.**
They show amateur and professional performers.

NEXT Think about live performance.

WHAT YOU HAVE TO WRITE

17. Write about an occasion when you

either took part in a live performance

or helped behind the scenes.

Remember to include your **thoughts and feelings.**

OR

18. Television shows such as *Pop Idol* do more harm than good.
Discuss.

OR

19. **Write a short story** using **ONE** of the following titles:

The Fame Game   Practice Makes Perfect

[Turn over for assignments 20 to 23 on *Page twelve*

There are no pictures for these assignments.

20. **Write a letter** using the following opening.

    Dear Sir/Madam,

    I am writing to complain in the strongest possible terms about . . .

OR

21. **Describe the scene** brought to mind by the following:

    "Scarring the very sky, they scrape and scratch ever upwards, those rectangles of glass and stone—our so modern office blocks."

OR

22. Letter-writing today is not dead; it has simply been updated by e-mail, texting and messaging.

    Discuss.

OR

23. **Write a short story** using **ONE** of the following openings.

    Make sure that you develop **character** and **setting** as well as **plot**.

    A cruel smile played on Kane's lips as he swung open the heavy door and stepped out into the cold, grim world . . .

    OR

    It was a misty morning in late November and Jane was late. Frantically late. She quickened her step . . .

    OR

    Tom was puzzled. Well, perhaps more perplexed than puzzled. He sat staring, wide-eyed, at the letter on the table . . .

[END OF QUESTION PAPER]

2006 Writing | Foundation | General | Credit

[BLANK PAGE]

Official SQA Past Papers: Foundation/General/Credit English 2006

FGC

0860/407

NATIONAL
QUALIFICATIONS
2006

WEDNESDAY, 3 MAY
9.00 AM – 10.15 AM

**ENGLISH
STANDARD GRADE**
Foundation, General
and Credit Levels
Writing

Read This First

1. Inside this booklet, there are photographs and words.
   Use them to help you when you are thinking about what to write.
   Look at all the material and think about all the possibilities.

2. There are 21 assignments altogether for you to choose from.

3. Decide which assignment you are going to attempt.
   Choose only **one** and write its number in the margin of your answer book.

4. Pay close attention to what you are asked to write.
   Plan what you are going to write.
   Read and check your work before you hand it in.
   Any changes to your work should be made clearly.

SCOTTISH
QUALIFICATIONS
AUTHORITY

SA 0860/407 6/67270

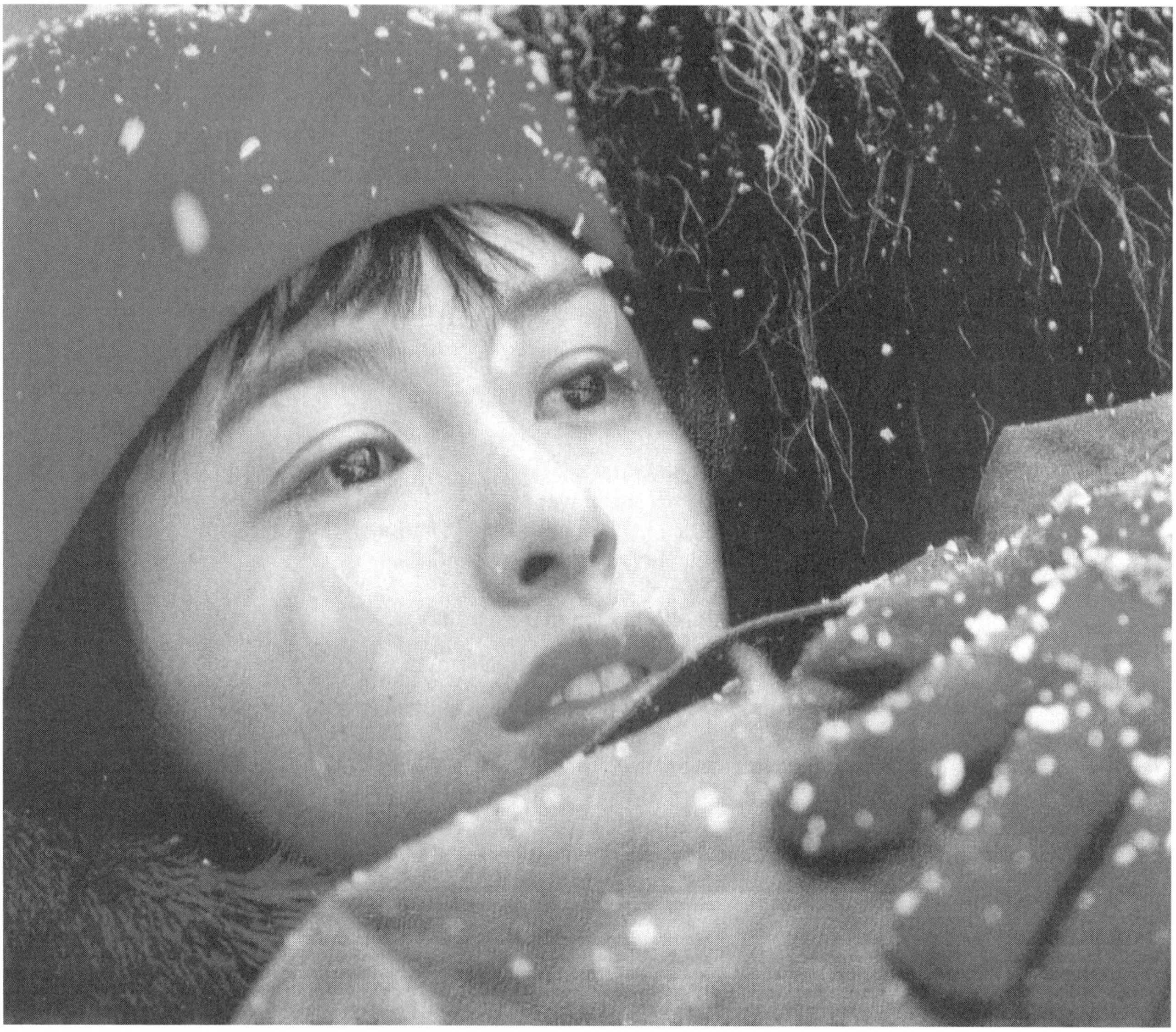

FIRST   **Look at the picture opposite.
It shows a couple parting.**

NEXT   Think how you might feel about leaving someone you care for.

WHAT YOU HAVE TO WRITE

1. **Write about** a time when you were separated from someone you cared about.

    You should concentrate on your **thoughts and feelings**.

    OR

2. **Write a short story** using the title:

    Never Forgotten.

    OR

3. We should be less afraid to speak openly about our feelings.

    Discuss.

    OR

4. **Write in any way you choose** using the picture opposite as your inspiration.

[Turn over

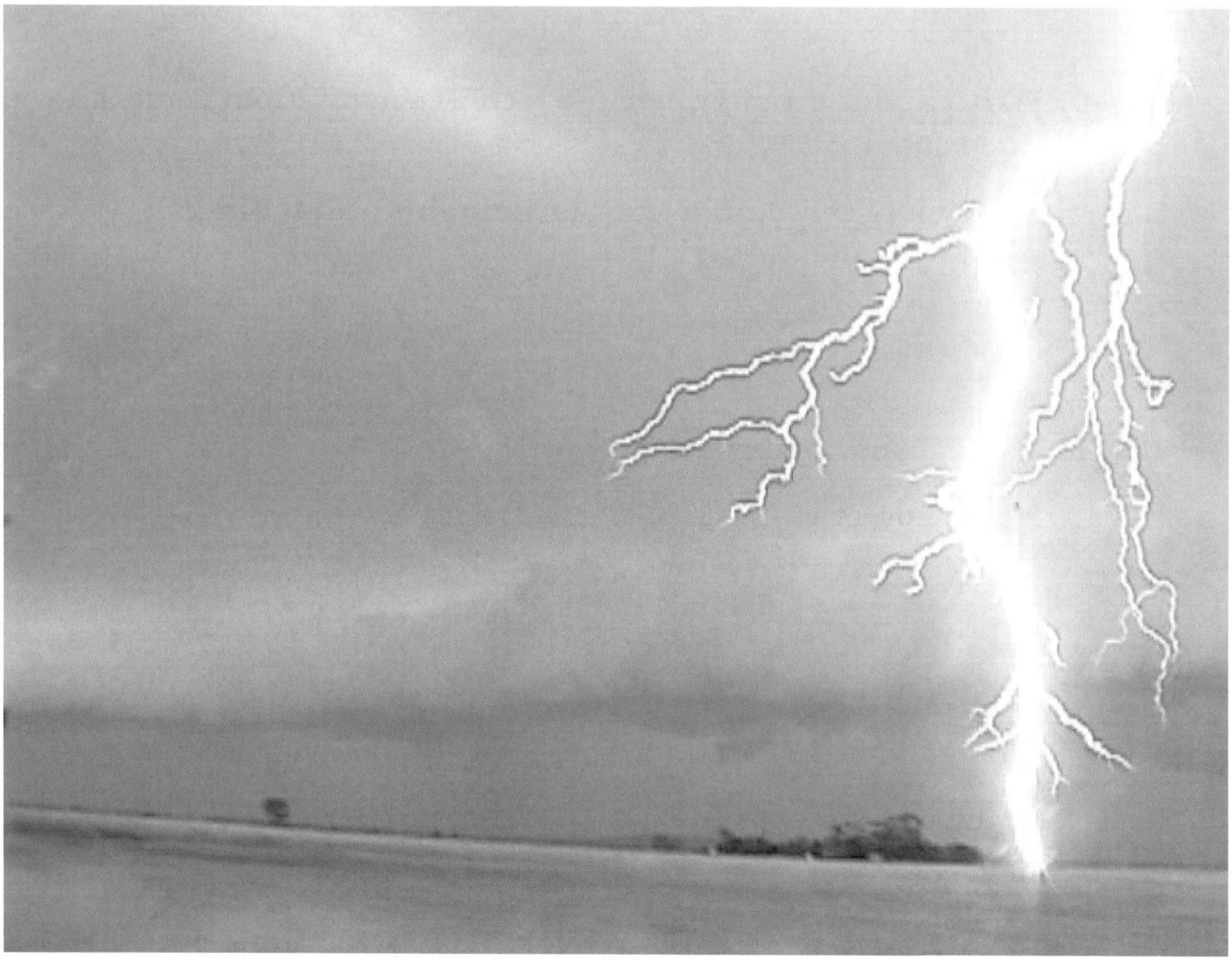

FIRST **Look at the picture opposite.
It shows a lightning strike.**

NEXT Think about the power of storms.

WHAT YOU HAVE TO WRITE

5. **Describe** both the excitement and the fear you experienced when you were caught in a storm.

    OR

6. **Write a short story** using **ONE** of the following titles:

    Stormchaser   Lightning Strikes Twice.

    OR

7. **Write a newspaper article** with the following headline:

    Storm Causes Widespread Damage.

    OR

8. Weather plays an important part in our everyday lives.
   Give your views.

[Turn over

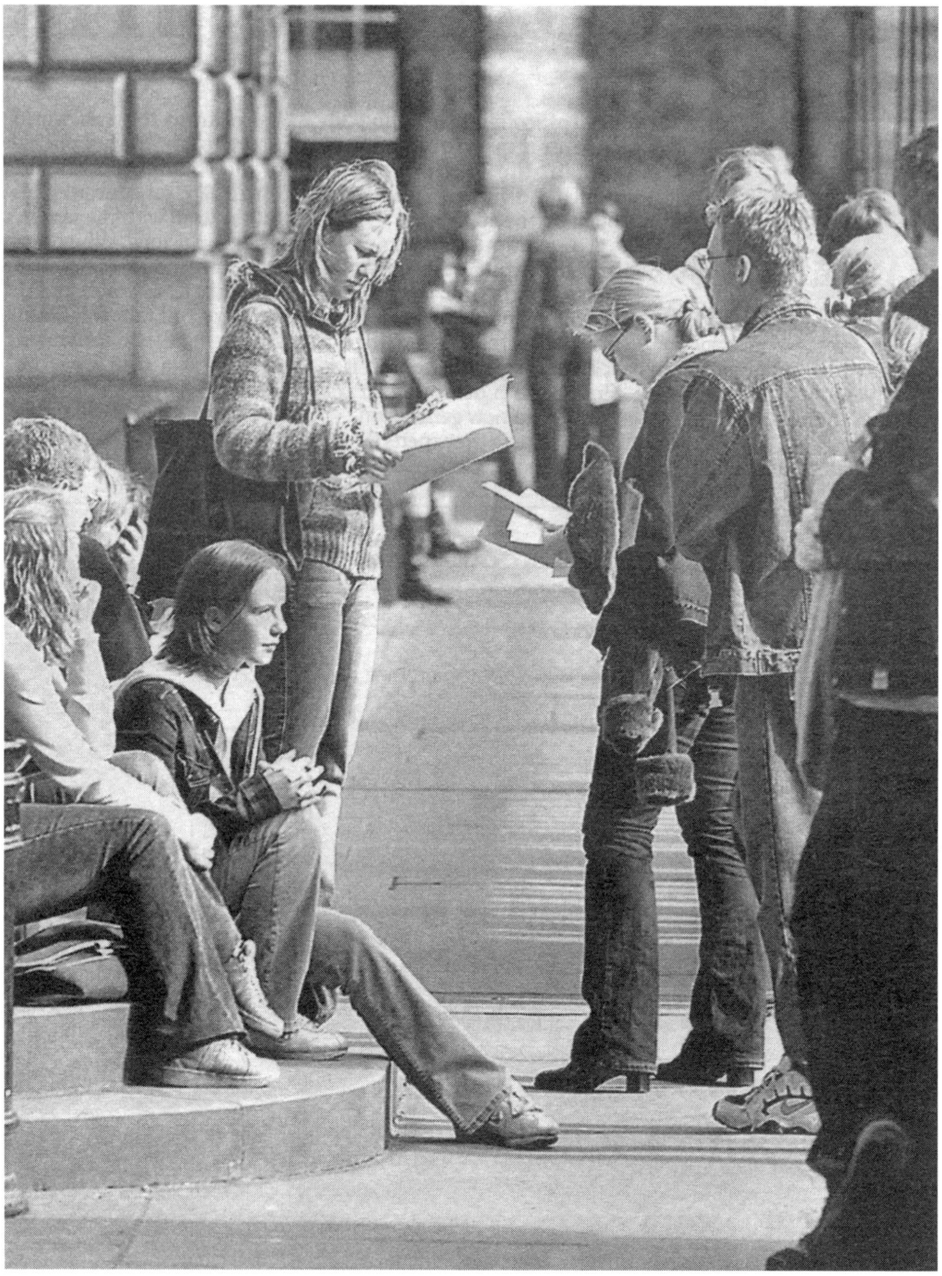

FIRST **Look at the picture opposite.
It shows a group of students.**

NEXT Think about life during and after school.

WHAT YOU HAVE TO WRITE

9. **Giving reasons**, write about your plans for when you leave school.

   OR

10. **Write a short story** using the following title:

    The Examination.

    OR

11. **Write an article** for your school magazine in which you describe the high points **and** the low points of your school years.

    OR

12. New places, new faces.

    Write about a time when you had to cope with new people in new surroundings.

    Remember to include your **thoughts and feelings**.

[Turn over

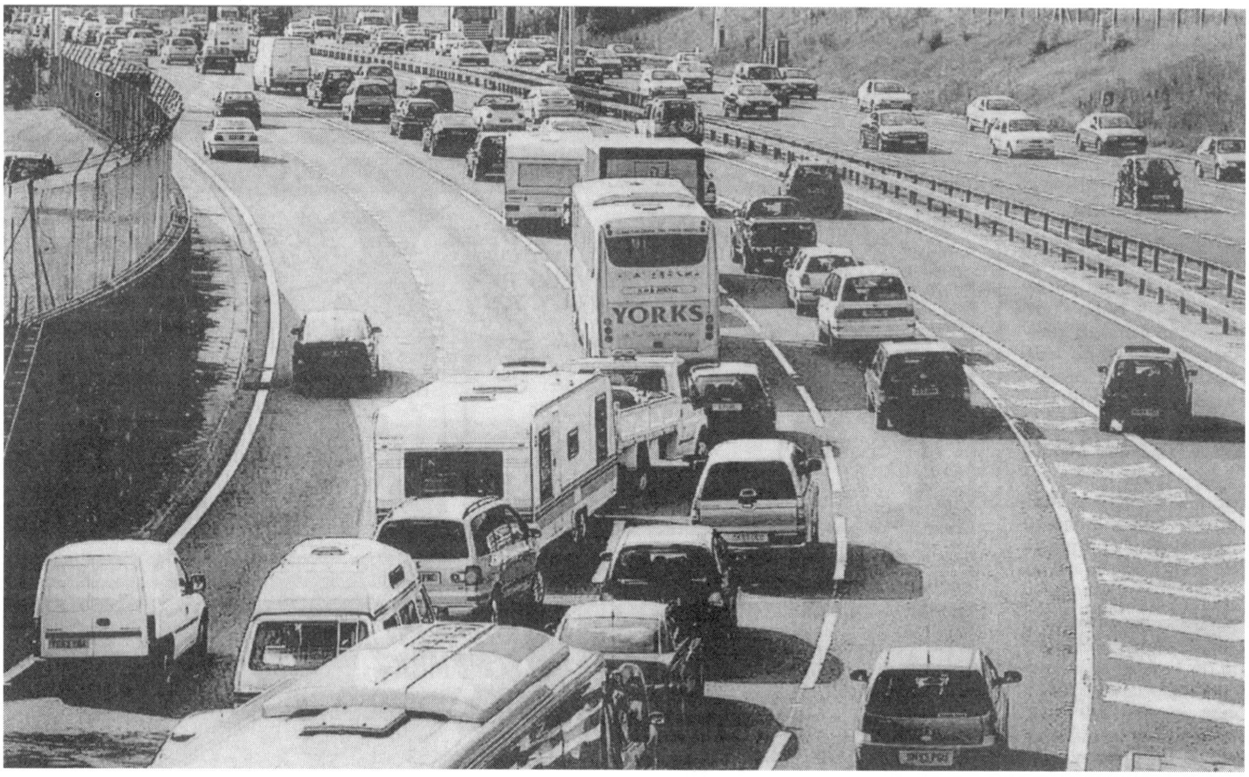
YORKS

FIRST **Look at the picture opposite.
It shows a traffic jam.**

NEXT Think about travel problems.

WHAT YOU HAVE TO WRITE

13. **Write about** an occasion when you were delayed during a journey. You should concentrate on your **thoughts and feelings**.

OR

14. **Write a short story** using the following title:

The Road to Nowhere.

OR

15. Road rage, air rage—the modern age.

Life today is simply too stressful.

Discuss.

[**Turn over**

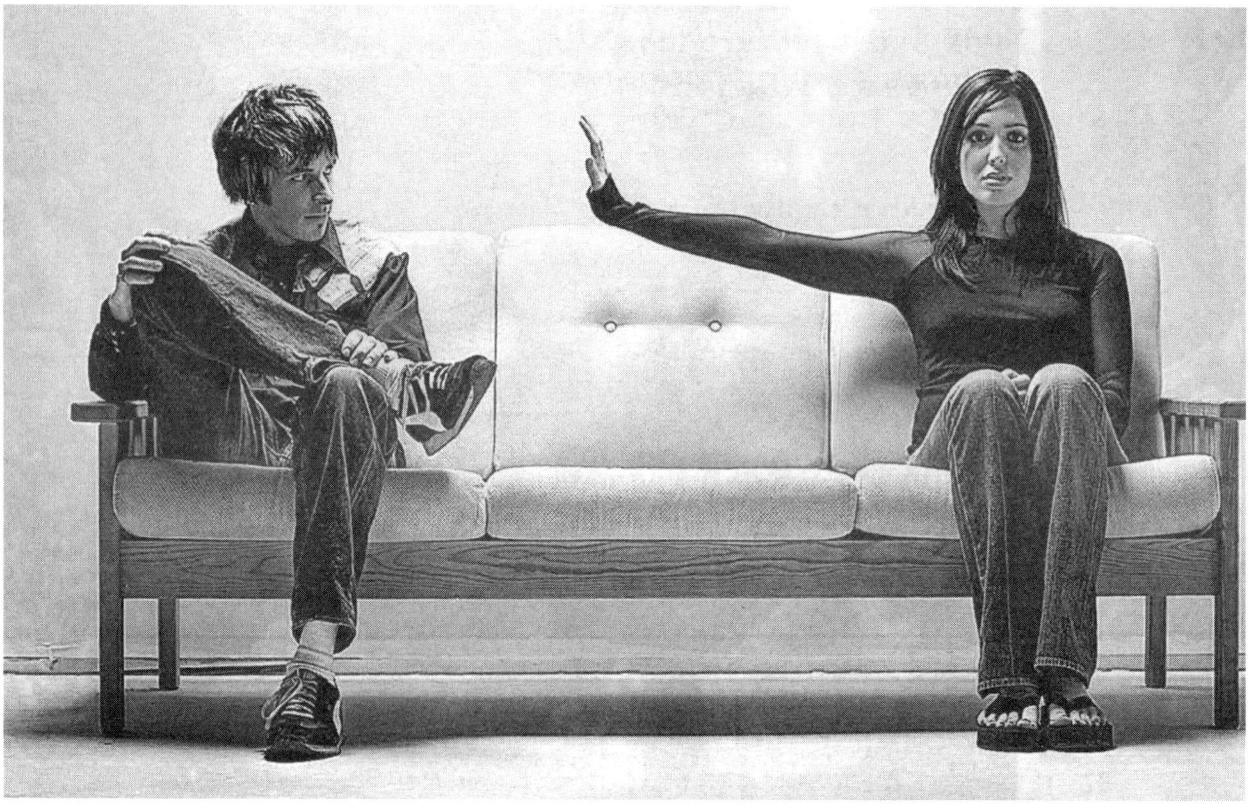

FIRST **Look at the picture opposite.**
It shows a young couple who have fallen out.

NEXT Think about relationships.

WHAT YOU HAVE TO WRITE

16. Write a short story using **ONE** of the following openings:

EITHER

Jill stared ahead intently, always away from him, focused firmly on the wall. He tried to speak. She raised her arm in protest . . .

OR

Andrew didn't know what to do. Just hours earlier things had been simply perfect. Now this. He let his mind wander back to . . .

OR

17. Magazines for young people do more good than harm.

Give your views.

OR

18. **Write about** your **thoughts and feelings** at a time when you were aware that someone simply wasn't listening.

[Turn over for assignments 19 to 21 on *Page twelve*

There are no pictures for these assignments.

19. **Write a short story** using the following opening.

    "He awoke in the ashes of a dead city. The cruel sun glared, showing neither pity nor mercy. He shook himself. It was no dream."

    Make sure that you develop **character** and **setting** as well as **plot**.

    OR

20. Look at me!

    Is it more important to be an individual or to fit in with the crowd?

    Discuss.

    OR

21. **Write a short story** using the title:

    Out of Time.

    Make sure that you develop **character** and **setting** as well as **plot**.

[END OF QUESTION PAPER]

2007 Writing | Foundation | General | Credit

0860/407

NATIONAL QUALIFICATIONS 2007

TUESDAY, 1 MAY 9.00 AM – 10.15 AM

ENGLISH
STANDARD GRADE
Foundation, General
and Credit Levels
Writing

Read This First

1 Inside this booklet, there are photographs and words.
 Use them to help you when you are thinking about what to write.
 Look at all the material and think about all the possibilities.

2 There are 23 assignments altogether for you to choose from.

3 Decide which assignment you are going to attempt.
 Choose only **one** and write its number in the margin of your answer book.

4 Pay close attention to what you are asked to write.
 Plan what you are going to write.
 Read and check your work before you hand it in.
 Any changes to your work should be made clearly.

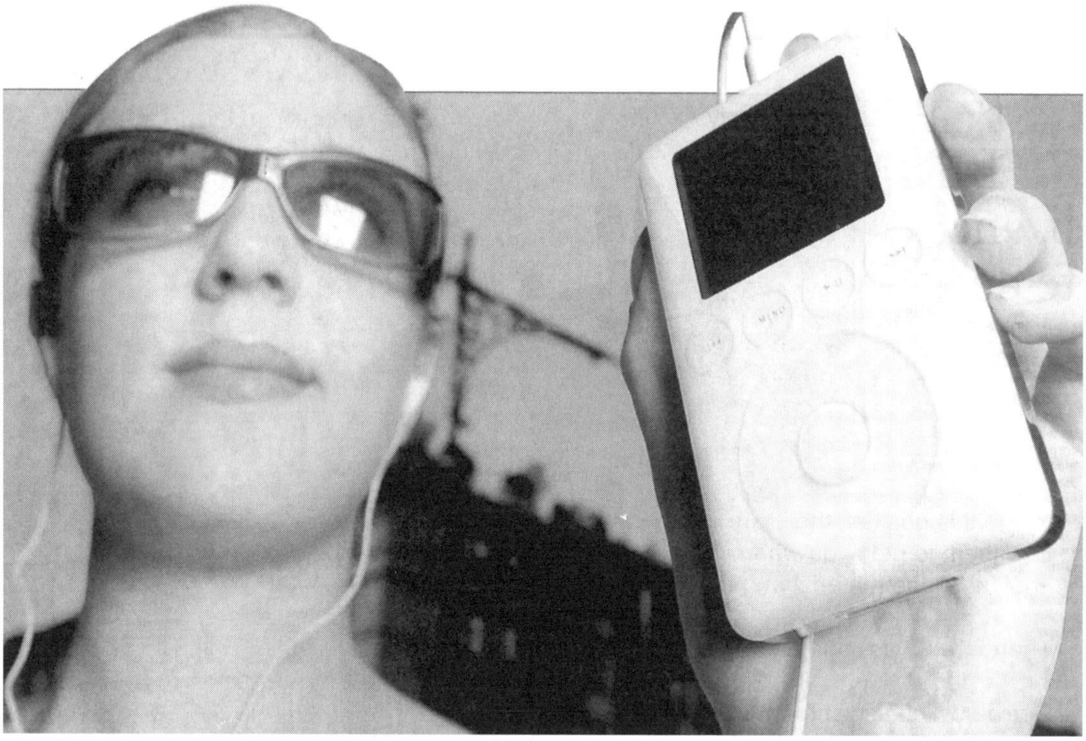

FIRST **Look at the picture opposite.
It shows a young woman with an MP3 player.**

NEXT Think about the importance of technology.

| WHAT YOU HAVE TO WRITE |

1. The one piece of technology I couldn't live without.

   Write about the importance to you of **ONE** piece of technology.

   OR

2. Young people today care too much for personal possessions.

   Give your views.

   OR

3. **Write a short story** using **ONE** of the following titles:

   Futureshock   She Saw the Future.

   You should develop **setting** and **character** as well as **plot**.

   [Turn over

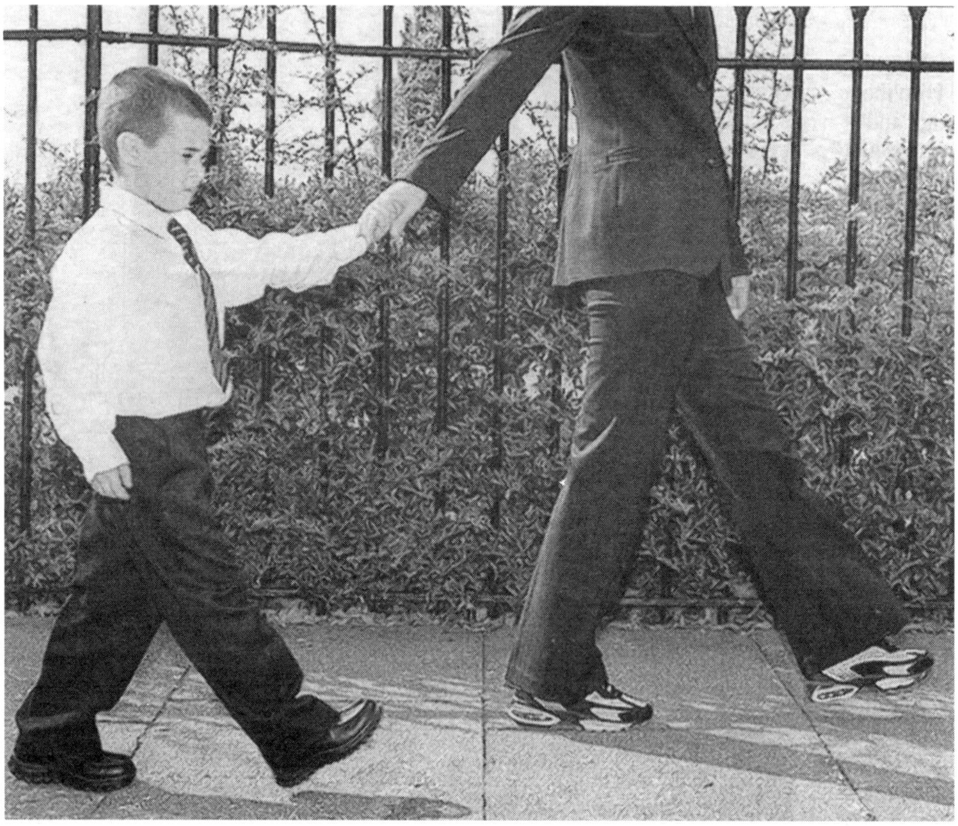

FIRST **Look at the picture opposite.**
       It shows a young boy being led by his mother.

NEXT   Think about your schooldays.

WHAT YOU HAVE TO WRITE

4. School Memories.

   Write about a person, place, or incident from your schooldays which you find unforgettable.

   Remember to include your **thoughts and feelings**.

   OR

5. **Write a short story** using the following opening:

   The reluctance was written all over John's face. He tugged at his mother's hand. He winced. He grimaced. He complained. Still his mother led him on . . .

   You should develop **setting** and **character** as well as **plot**.

   OR

6. All pupils should wear school uniform.

   Give your views.

[Turn over

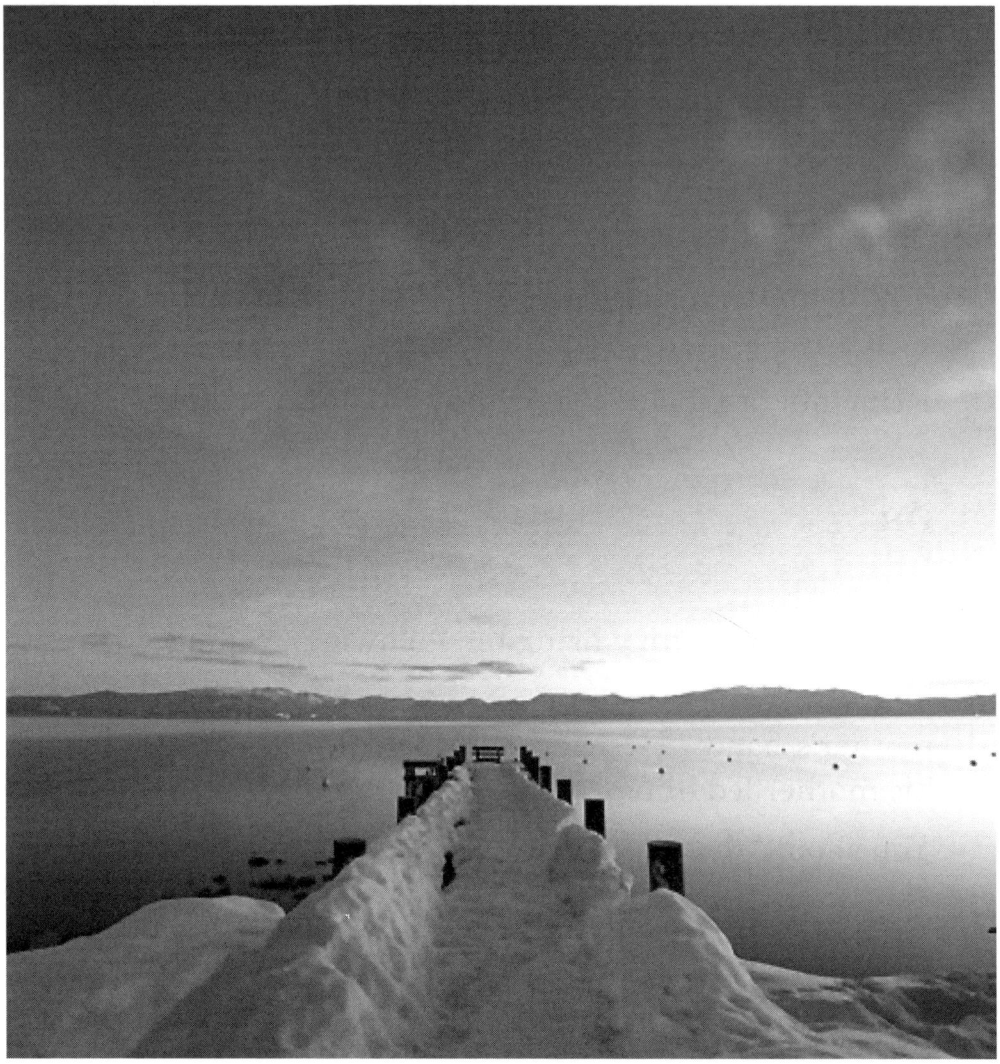

FIRST **Look at the picture opposite.**
It shows a lake in winter.

NEXT Think about special places.

WHAT YOU HAVE TO WRITE

7. Sometimes a special place can inspire us.

Write about such a place.

Remember to include your **thoughts and feelings**.

OR

8. Write in any way you choose using the picture opposite as your inspiration.

OR

9. Write about a time when you were alone but happy.

You should concentrate on your **thoughts and feelings**.

OR

10. Write an informative article for a travel magazine titled:

The Best Holiday Destination For Young People.

[Turn over

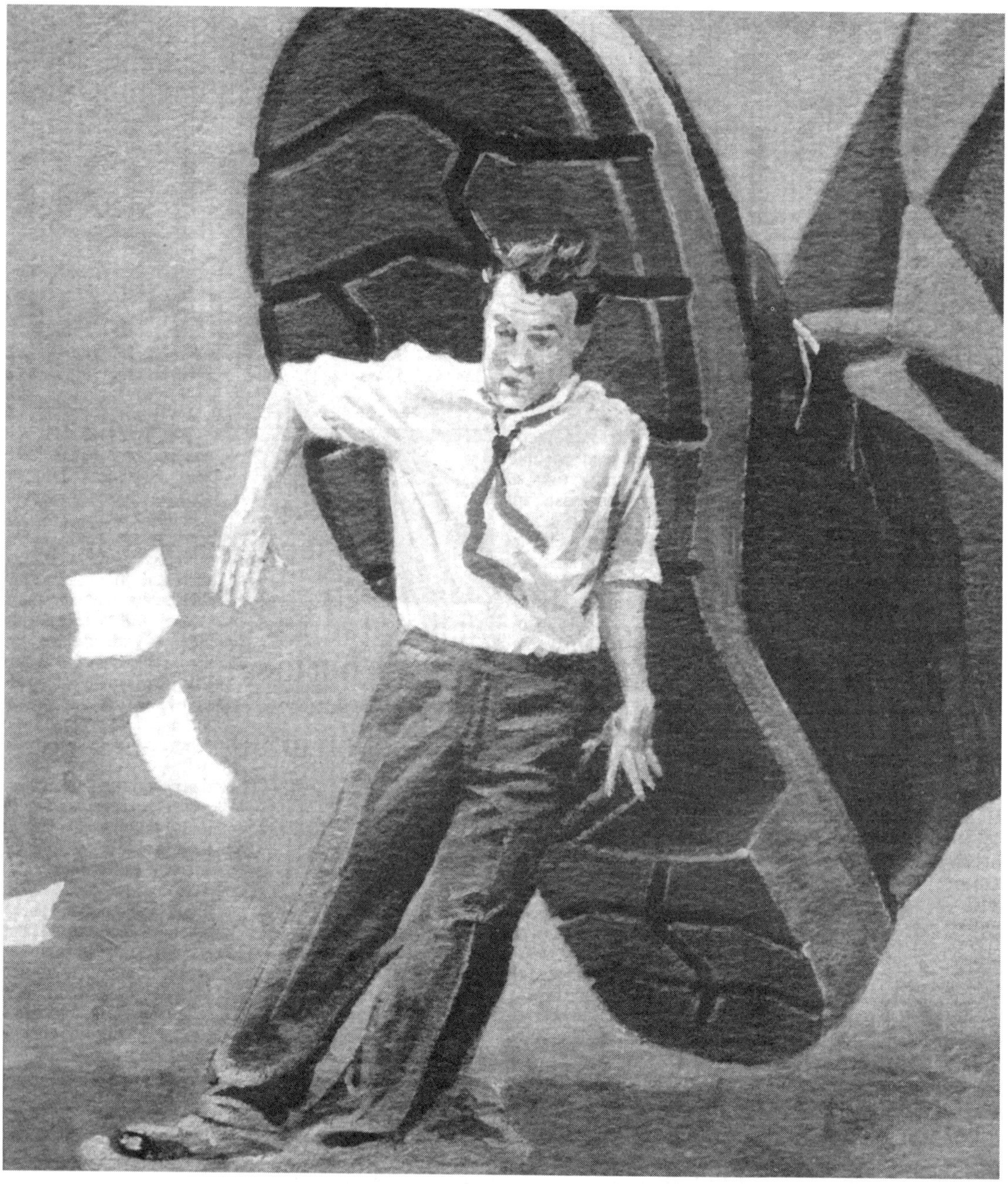

FIRST   **Look at the picture opposite.**
        It shows a man under pressure.

NEXT   Think about the pressures of life.

| WHAT YOU HAVE TO WRITE |

11. **Write about** a time in your life when you had to face personal pressure.

    You should describe your **thoughts and feelings**.

    OR

12. **Write a short story** using **ONE** of the following titles:

    The Underdog   Free at Last.

    You should develop **setting** and **character** as well as **plot**.

    OR

13. It's Just Not Fair!

    Write about an occasion when you took a stand against injustice.

    You should concentrate on your **thoughts and feelings** as well as what you did.

    OR

14. These days young people are unfairly treated by the media.

    Give your views.

    [Turn over

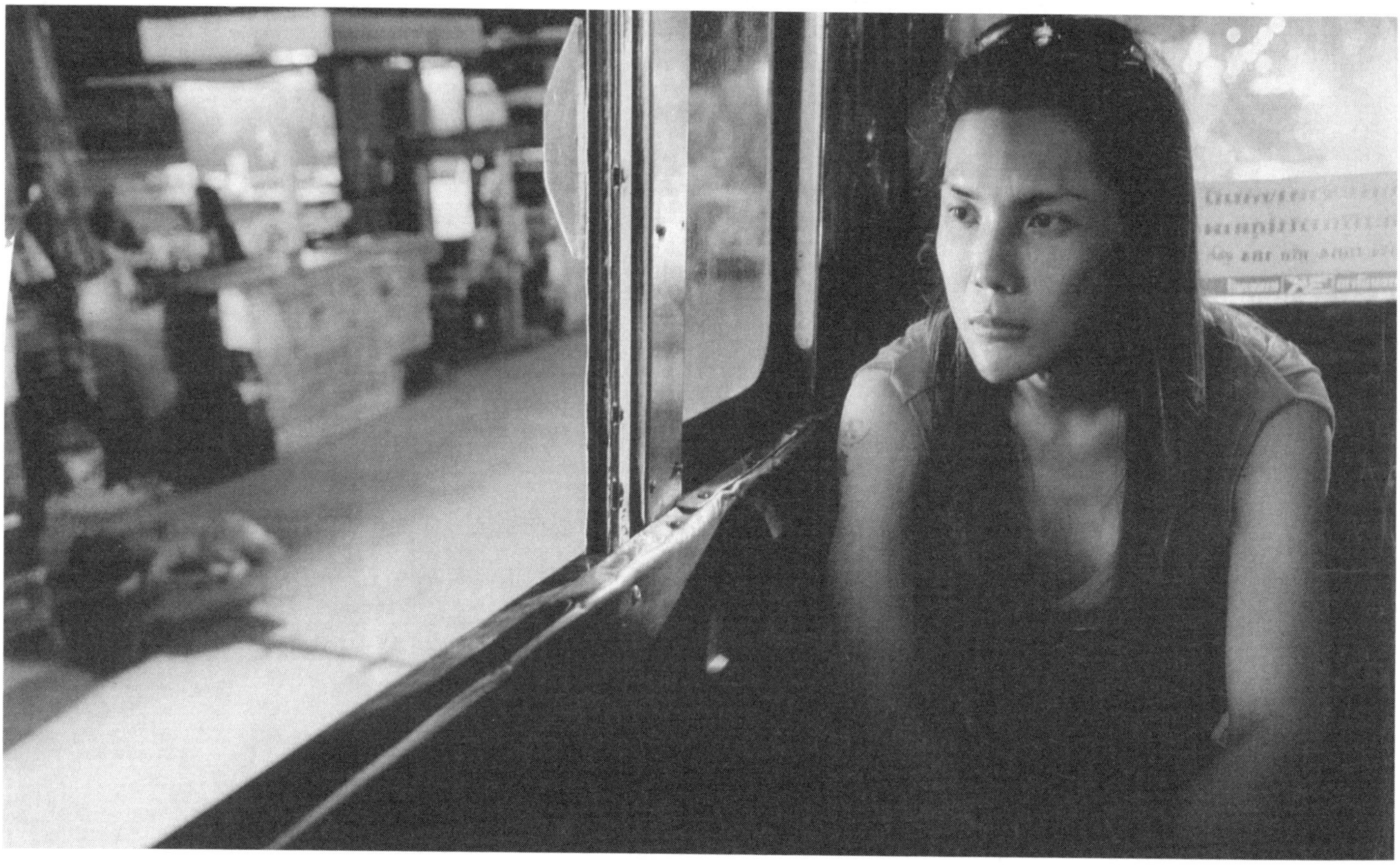

FIRST   **Look at the picture opposite.**
It shows a young woman on a bus, alone with her thoughts.

NEXT   Think about moments of reflection.

WHAT YOU HAVE TO WRITE

15. "The glass is always half full; never half empty."

It is important to have a positive outlook on life.

Give your views.

OR

16. **Write about** an occasion when you had an unpleasant duty to perform.

You should concentrate on your **thoughts and feelings**.

OR

17. Act Your Age!

There are fewer chances today simply to be yourself.

Give your views.

OR

18. **Write a short story** using **ONE** of the following titles:

Stranger in a Strange Land   No Return.

You should develop **setting** and **character** as well as **plot**.

[Turn over for assignments 19 to 23 on *Page twelve*

There are no pictures for these assignments.

19. We should try to solve the problems here on earth before we spend more on space exploration.

    Give your views.

    OR

20. **Describe the scene** brought to mind by the following:

    A stark land of leafless trees and merciless wind.

    OR

21. We forget our past at our peril!

    Not enough is being done to keep Scottish heritage alive.

    Write a newspaper article in which you give your views on this topic.

    OR

22. There are special times of the year when people celebrate in their own way.

    Describe such a special time, bringing out its importance to you, your family, and your community.

    OR

23. **Write a short story** using the following title:

    The Traveller.

    You should develop **setting** and **character** as well as **plot**.

[*END OF QUESTION PAPER*]

[BLANK PAGE]

[BLANK PAGE]

[BLANK PAGE]

[BLANK PAGE]

Acknowledgements

Leckie and Leckie is grateful to the copyright holders, as credited, for permission to use their material:
'We're out for the Count' by Catriona Marchant © *The Times*, London, 13 October 2001 (2003 General Reading paper p 2);
Allstar Picture Library for a photograph (2003 Writing paper p 6);
The Mail on Sunday for the article 'Pucker way to kiss a hummingbird' by Mark Carwardine (2004 General Reading paper p 2);
The BBC for a photograph (2004 General Reading paper p 2);
Getty Images for a photograph (2004 Writing paper p 2);
Getty Images for a photograph (2004 Writing paper p 8);
Camera Press, London, for a photograph by John Swannell (2004 Writing paper p 10);
The Sunday Times for the article 'Dazzling the Stars' by John Harlow (2005 General Reading paper p 2);
FreeFoto.com for a photograph (2005 Writing paper p 4);
The Scotsman for a photograph (2005 Writing paper p 6);
Ralph A. Clevenger/Corbis for a photograph (2005 Writing paper p 8);
Telegraph Group Limited for the article 'Ain't No Mountain High Enough' by Deborah Netburn, taken from *The Sunday Telegraph Magazine* 27 June 2004 (2006 Foundation Reading paper p 2);
Getty/Matthew Cavanaugh for the photograph '77th Scripps Howard Spelling Bee Enters Final Round' (2006 General Reading paper p 2);
The Scotsman for the photograph 'Scots will be squeezed out. Fee Refugees!' (2006 Writing paper p 6);
Design Pics Inc./Alamy for the photograph 'People' (2006 Writing paper p 10).
Express Newspapers for an article from *The Sunday Express*: 'Why dumped dog is such a lucky hound' by David Wigg (2007 Foundation Reading paper p 2);
Rex Features Ltd for the photograph 'iPod Generation' by Dan Callister (2007 Writing paper p 2);
Getty Images for a photograph (2007 Writing paper p 4);
Dan Heller for the photograph from www.danheller.com (2007 Writing paper p 6);
Getty Images for a photograph by David Hogsholt (2007 Writing paper p 10);
Telegraph Group Limited for the article 'The Fabulous Biker Boys (and Girls)' by John Dodd, taken from *The Sunday Telegraph Magazine* 28th August 2005 (2007 General Reading paper p 2).

The following companies have very generously given permission to reproduce their copyright material free of charge:
FreeFoto.com for 4 photographs (2003 Writing paper pp 2, 4, 8 & 10);
Maurice Lacroix Ltd for an advertisement (2004 Writing paper p 4);
Newsquest Media Group for a photograph (2004 Writing paper p 4);
News Team International for a photograph (2004 Writing paper p 6);
The House of Lochar Publishers for an extract from *Think Me Back* by Catherine Forde (2005 Foundation Reading paper pp 2-4);
Newsquest Media Group for a photograph (2005 Writing paper p 10);
TES Scotland for a photograph (2005 Writing paper p 10);
Pearson Education for an extract from *You Don't Know Me* by David Klass (2006 General Reading paper pp 2-4);
Newsquest Media Group for the photograph 'Stretching the Nerves' by Kieran Dodds (2006 Writing paper p 8);